Basic Tools for Beginning Writers

How to teach all the skills beginning writers need—from alphabet recognition and spelling to strategies for self-editing and building coherent text

Betty Schultze

Pembroke Publishers Limited

Dedicated to my grandchildren
Maia Ferguson, Sebastian Pango, and Cole Checkwitch

Pembroke Publishers
538 Hood Road
Markham, Ontario, Canada L3R 3K9
www.pembrokepublishers.com

Distributed in the U.S. by Stenhouse Publishers
480 Congress Street
Portland, ME 04101
www.stenhouse.com

We acknowledge the financial support of the Government of Canada through the Book Publishing Industry Development Program (BPIDP) for our publishing activities.

We acknowledge the Government of Ontario through the Ontario Media Development Corporation's Ontario Book Initiative.

Library and Archives Canada Cataloguing in Publication

Schultze, Betty
Basic tools for beginning writers / Betty Schultze.

Includes index.
ISBN 978-1-55138-221-0

1. English language—Composition and exercises—Study and teaching (Primary). 2. English language—Writing—Study and teaching (Primary). I. Title.

LB1528.S363 2008   372.62'3044   C2007-906737-9

Editor: Kate Revington
Cover Design: John Zehethofer
Typesetting: Jay Tee Graphics Ltd.

Printed and bound in Canada
9 8 7 6 5 4 3 2 1

Contents

Overview: A Contextual Framework *5*

Beliefs about Teaching Basic Writing Skills *6*
Recognizing Different Levels of Readiness *9*
When to Teach Basic Tools *10*
How to Set Up the Classroom *11*
Involving All Students in Learning *12*
Setting Appropriate Expectations *13*
Ways to Assess Basic Skills *14*
Keeping in Touch with the Home *15*

1. Putting Pencil to Paper *17*

How to Hold a Pencil Correctly *18*
Printing Names *22*
Making Simple Pictures *28*

2. Identifying and Making Letters of the Alphabet *37*

Alphabet Stories *38*
Six Alphabet Stations *43*
Using Alphabet Books, Raps, and Jives *46*

3. Incorporating Basic Tools into Routines and Play *57*

The Morning Message *57*
Stage One: Two Lines of Print *59*
Stage Two: Introducing Cloze *59*
Stage Three: Guiding Practice *60*
Stage Four: Communicating through Cloze *62*
Ways to Provide Variety to Morning Message *62*
Writing in Centres *64*
The Blocks Centre *65*
The Home Centre *66*
The Easels Centre *67*
The Post Office Centre *68*
Literacy Centres *68*

4. Phonemic Awareness and Sound–Symbol Matches *70*

Phoneme, Word, or Sentence? *71*
Ghost Talk — Learning to Separate the Phonemes in Simple Words *74*
The Bumping Game — Blending Two Phonemes Together *78*
Using Elkonin Boxes with Prompts *81*

5. Learning How to Spell *91*

Read It! Write It! *92*
Working with Word Families — The Power of Onset and Rime *95*
Creating a Weekly Spelling List *99*

6. Creating a Legible, Coherent Text *108*

Printing Legibly on Lines *109*
Learning about Capitals and Periods *111*
Doing a Simple Self-Edit *112*
Writing a Longer Story — Ways to Increase Volume *117*

Recommended Resources *127*
Appendixes *128*
Index *132*
Acknowledgments *136*

Overview: A Contextual Framework

The pre-Kindergarten child sees her mother adding items to the grocery list and soon she finds a pencil and a piece of paper and enthusiastically begins to create her own list. She has lots of ideas: a cereal she especially loves, apples, and bananas, but when she goes to write the words, a puzzled look appears. "How do you write that?" she asks.

"You'll learn all about how to write those words at school," her mother confidently assures her. "For now, just do some pretend writing, and we'll read it together."

This child will learn how to write those words at school. She will learn how to make pictures that tell stories and very soon how to turn the talk of stories into written words. Much of this will happen as the teacher describes every student who makes any kind of graphic representation on paper as a writer. The teacher encourages students to take the next step in the writing process, whether it is putting more details into their pictures or printing "pretend" letters under a picture. Along with positively confirming what students already do in their writing, and nudging them along the continuum with prompts, good teachers help students think about story and how to craft their thoughts into good writing. Many of these steps are presented in *What's Next for This Beginning Writer?* (see Recommended Resources). Taking students from scribbles to script, it focuses on teaching children to think about **what** they can write and on how to encourage them to proceed.

The focus of *Basic Tools for Beginning Writers* is on a complementary, but different aspect of teaching writing: teaching students the basic writing tools that ensure they will know **how** to write. A basic writing tool is defined here as a skill that students need in order to be able to do both the physical and mental tasks to produce legible words on paper. Students need to learn how to grasp the pencil, print legibly, spell, punctuate, and create sentences. To teach this effectively, teachers need to be familiar with best practices in developing writing competency. These practices include knowing how to teach students such different skills as the fine motor skills needed to form letters, words, and sentences in pencil and the ability to see the relationship between phonemes and the letters that make up our alphabet system. The lessons may seem simple, but they are essential, and sometimes, they are not taught effectively. Through identifying basic skills and expanding on them with background information, lesson ideas, suggestions for student review, and ways to make lessons both simpler and more challenging, this book will provide the tools to help students become better writers.

For a moment, let's make a comparison that helps illustrate the difference between teaching students the strategies and approaches that will help them better craft their writing and teaching them the skills to write words on paper.

Imagine the work that goes into the building of a beautiful home and compare it to the work of creating a well-written piece of text. Before the carpenter estimates the lumber needed, pounds a first nail, or frames up a foundation, the concept of the house needs to be established and blueprinted plans completed. The plans of the house, including the site references and layout of the rooms, are like the content of a story. To get to their prospective finished pieces, however, both the carpenter and the writer must be familiar with a number of tools and have practice using them. For the carpenter, that includes the ability to use both power tools and things as simple as a hammer. He needs to know how to frame windows, how to create forms for concrete, what nails to use and where. A writer, too, needs skills to go beyond thinking up ideas for a story to tell or considering facts to share. A beginning writer needs to know how to use basic phonemic and alphabetic tools to produce words and sentences that are legible enough to be read and understood. A writer needs practice in everything from writing letters quickly, to separating the phonemes in a word, to learning how to edit.

This resource guides teachers through a continuum of lessons and classroom routines that provide a fun, effective way to teach beginning writers how to write their stories, share their facts, and express their opinions. It emphasizes the core of what needs to be taught to beginning writers and will help students learn the Basic Tools quickly so that they can get on with their writing.

Basic Tools for Beginning Writers is based on the contextual framework outlined in the pages that follow. It is a resource for Kindergarten, Grade 1, and Grade 2 classroom teachers, Resource teachers who work with children of all ages who have special needs, Reading Assistance teachers, and teachers of all English Language Learner (ELL) students. It is also a useful resource for Special Education assistants who work with students one on one or with small groups of students with special needs.

Beliefs about Teaching Basic Writing Skills

Three important beliefs about the best way to teach young children basic writing skills are outlined below. These beliefs may guide your practice:

Children learn to write through writing.

During Writing Workshop, a designated time for all students to write about personal experiences, students will do their best learning about writing. Invite students to take part in the act of writing by putting a pencil or crayon in their hands, putting paper in front of them, providing encouragement, and asking them to write a story. For some students this will be a jerky scribble created by a ham-fisted grasp of a fat crayon; for others it will be a detailed picture sketch of recognizable objects with an explanation or a personal narrative.

At this time, students learn to use models to further their writing craft. These models are both teacher based, through small- or whole-group lessons where the teacher demonstrates what is expected, and student based, through student examples the teacher uses to demonstrate specific aspects of writing craft. The teacher will descriptively mirror back to a child the skills the child exhibits, even if sometimes it's just "Wow! You made a nice red mark on this paper! That's what writers do — make their marks on paper."

But in order to prepare the students for Writing Workshop, the teacher will also need to find time to teach beginning writers basic writing conventions. As children write personal narratives, poems, and non-fiction pieces, they are doing the independent practice needed for printing, spelling, and punctuation to become more standard and less inventive in nature. This transition will happen in a gradual way, but it is a mistake to rely totally on time and experience to ensure that changes will occur or to believe that children need constant prompting and reminders about conventions when they write. Students need direct instruction on such things as how to hold a pencil, how to make some shapes and pictures, and how to put sounds and letters together in a way that enables them to create legible script. Generally, these lessons are done outside of Writing Workshop time, and these lessons are the focus of this book.

Children learn best when they are experiencing success.

Vygotsky called the learning environment where students can be successfully challenged without frustration the zone of proximal development. In this zone, instruction appropriate to each child's needs must be focused. Although teachers may prepare lessons that seem appropriate for all students in the class, some students will need much more practice than others or may not be ready to even tackle the skill, and some students will not need the lesson at all.

Throughout this book, there are many suggestions on adapting lessons for students who may not learn as quickly as others. There has also been an attempt to make the lessons fun to do even if the child has already mastered the skill. In this way, more capable students can enjoy the game aspect of a lesson while practising basic skills and learning the language related to these skill sets; less capable students can do a modified version of the lesson. Consistent repetition of some concepts will provide many opportunities for students to gain understanding at their unique developmental rates.

When teachers reflect "out loud" on the learning that has taken place with the students and support their attempts and successes, students will see themselves as competent learners. Here are some typical comments that teachers might make to students during the practice part of a lesson:

"Jacob, you have made such nice straight lines, and I really love the way these two *t*'s [pointing to two well-made *t*'s] have the second line just the right size, centred and not too big or too small."

"You and your friend Jessie bumped together these two sounds: /r/ and /o/. You made the word *row* together. No one else thought of that — it's a clever word. Good for you!"

"Jackie, you looked at the crab and when you used your counters to move it and say it, you found the word had four phonemes. What smart ears you have! You are listening for every phoneme."

By focusing on what students are doing correctly, providing language that clearly labels the learning, and then giving a simple prompt to encourage further exploration, teachers can ensure that students are motivated, feeling successful, and working in the zone of proximal development.

Modeling, as part of direct instruction, is an important part of teaching.

Modeling is the best way to teach the simple skills that all students need. This means that you always consider the four steps of modeling in each lesson. Below is one way to remember the steps of modeling:

1. I show you; you watch and listen.
2. I show you; you help me.
3. You show me; I help you.
4. You show me; I watch and listen.

These steps are also the basis for guided practice and finally independent practice, important parts of learning a skill.

Below is an example of how modeling might look during Morning Message, a common teaching time for children to learn about reading and writing in a Kindergarten or Grade 1 classroom.

First, you would write a sentence or two on the board and model by talking out loud about what you are doing, for example:

"I'm going to write a sentence on this big piece of paper for you. I am going to start at the top and on the left-hand side of the page. I am going to say, 'Good morning, boys and girls,' but I'm going to write my talk down and that makes it something to read. I start with a big letter for my /ggg/ sound in 'Good morning' and then I write the whole word. Between each letter there are some little spaces that a piece of spaghetti could fit between but I have to put a whole 'meatball' space between words. Meatballs are big, but not too big." [You might have a meatball of modeling clay as a concrete example.] "At the end of the sentence, I will make a dot, which we call a period. That tells the reader that the sentence is finished."

Obviously, there is a lot to say about even a five-word sentence and it's important that children don't spend all their time listening. Even with daily modeling of the same sentence, each day you will comment on something new and not try to make every teaching point possible. As you model how talk is written down, the students are learning about the conventions of print. This is the "I show you and you watch" part of modeling.

After several days of modeling, you may ask for help from the students. In the first weeks of modeling a Morning Message in Kindergarten, it is helpful to begin with the same sentence. Soon you can ask: "Where do I start to write? What letter makes the sound /g/? What kind of space do I need between words — a spaghetti space or a meatball space?" Observant children can help you and answer questions, or for more active student involvement, ask all students to make the letter in the air, answer in unison, or whisper the answer to the person beside them. This is the "I show you and you help me" part of modeling.

It will not be long before you can ask a student to fill in missing letters as you put up a Morning Message. You can create some empty spaces, such as in this example:

_ood _orning _oys and _irls

You can leave out periods and capitals, and students will come up and write the missing letters for you; or, you can write the letters and blanks on a sheet for duplication or on an individual chalkboard. In this way, students are doing the task but with significant help from you. This is the "You show me and I help you" part of modeling.

Eventually, students can write the sentence "Good morning, boys and girls" on their own, although this degree of independence will not happen for some time.

Recognizing Different Levels of Readiness

It is well accepted that all young children develop at different rates. Some children are ready for formal instruction about the phonographic system or have the fine motor abilities to make letters with a pencil before other children.

A cardinal rule of good teaching is to start where the child is, which means that if a child needs to grasp a thick pencil or crayon in an appropriate way in order to make a mark, then that is the place to start. Nonetheless, it is important to provide some scaffolding to ensure that the child can attempt the next, more sophisticated step and to provide plenty of practice and support. There will always be some students for whom you will need to simplify your lessons so that they can succeed. The topics and lesson ideas in this book follow a rough continuum so that the easiest skills come first. It is essential to make continuous observations and to record the progress of each student.

Marie Clay, the founder of the Reading Recovery program, has taught that children can learn to read without knowing all the letters of the alphabet; similarly, it is important that students attempt to learn Basic Tools without necessarily having mastered a preceding skill. For example, a child may not be able to write her name independently, but can still practise isolating phonemes in saying names in Ghost Talk (outlined on pages 74–78) or print capital and lowercase *S*'s as she works on making letters. With much repetition and use of innovative ways to approach a skill, students will learn.

The teacher's attitude towards learning is also an important ingredient in how young children get motivated to learn a skill. My colleagues and I have found that when teachers adopt the belief that "Every child is a reader!" and understand that their job is to ensure that students, regardless of readiness level, are faced with text and expectations to read every day, reading progress in classrooms is remarkable. Teachers teach the students at a level where they can be successful by providing appropriate simple text and specific learning goals, such as finding the beginnings of words and matching words and pictures. Careful observation of what a child can do dictates the next step in the learning process, but each step is carefully taught, using modeling, lots of practice, encouragement, prompting, and praise. This type of teaching is in contrast to a time when teachers believed that children would read when they were ready and then waited for a "readiness" that for some children never appeared! For some children a lack of instruction at the beginning of the learning process can have disastrous results. Every child deserves to be taught carefully and guided with high expectations for eventual success.

When teachers believe that "Every student is a writer!" we start students on their writing journey. The path to writing ability is through respect of a child's ability at the moment, systematic direct instruction at the appropriate instructional level, teacher support for student effort, and many opportunities for practice and consolidation. Except for those with disabilities, the children in our classes will most certainly become writers if we follow this process.

When to Teach Basic Tools

Writing Workshop is the time when students create stories, poems, and lists, and do the real work of writing by exploring topics, drawing, drafting, and perhaps even revising. Direct instruction in various aspects of writing craft is given in mini-lessons at the beginning of the time allotted. In these brief lessons, students are taught and encouraged on how to add details, stretch out a personal moment, label items in their pictures with first-letter labels, create poems, and more.

Teaching the Basic Tools for beginning writers deserves its own time for instruction. It should not be during Writing Workshop or during the writing times that are part of play, science, literature response, and the like. Basic writing tools can be taught as part of a daily routine, such as Morning Message, or as part of a learning or literacy centre where a group of students work with a teacher or teacher's aide around a table. Sometimes, the lesson can be taught to the whole class in a literacy time usually devoted to learning about words, where spelling and graphophonemic skills are taught. (Graphophonemic skills relate to the process of hearing and recording sounds in words accurately.) Some of these skills can also be taught while students are doing the writing part of their lesson in guided reading groups. Lessons of 10 to 15 minutes work well.

The Basic Tools lessons provide language that can be used any time students are writing. Opportunities to reinforce the lessons happen as the teacher comments on writing activities during centre times, science, and other times in the day. Some comments might be as follows:

"Mary, you did such an excellent job of writing this menu! You have written 'bakin' and 'egs' and I can read it because it has all the sounds in it. You have listened for all the phonemes in *bacon* and *eggs*. Good for you!"

"Ajepaul, you are such a brave and fearless speller! You have made a sign that I can read. It says, "LINS GAT BRIJ" and you even included capital letters to show how the names of things have capitals!"

"I love your sentence about the observation you made about your bean plant, Harmen. It is so easy to read because you have put spaces between your words and it says, 'My plant is 7 cm hi.' Good remembering!"

In active primary classrooms, writing takes place all day long. Children are writing in response to literature, writing to observe what is happening in science, writing to report solutions to problems they ponder in personal planning sessions, or creating signs and menus for traditional play centres. Although the focus is not on learning graphophonemic skills or editing during these times, the writing provides opportunities for students to practise creating words, punctuating sentences, and printing letters with appropriate shapes and sizes.

How to Set Up the Classroom

A teaching centre with supplies and materials that can work easily for whole-group or for small-group instruction at the carpet is recommended. By having felt pens, white tape for errors, and chart paper and chalk or white board space handy, you reduce the time needed to set up your lesson.

Like most Kindergarten and early primary teachers, I like to have students sitting at the carpet for instruction. Students often sit in a semi-circle or sometimes two rough semi-circles in front of me.

Many Kindergarten teachers print the names of students or student "partner pairs" on masking tape at the places where they will sit. This practice ensures that students who do not listen well are sitting close to you and those who may prefer talking to each other rather than listening to you are not sitting close to each other.

After some time in school, students will become accustomed to the routines for carpet time and will come when you signal, ready for instruction. Early in the year, teach them partner behaviors. When you post names with those of partners for a week somewhere the pairs can easily see, it not only helps students learn names quickly, but allows you to match students you think can work well together.

At your teaching centre, be sure to have a sizable empty space on your chalkboard or whiteboard as well as chart paper ready for writing. You need to be able to "talk with your chalk." Students need consistent exposure to print, and when you write down ideas, sketch diagrams, make lists and messages, and create stories for pictures, it is writing in action.

Students need both visual and oral stimulation to help them understand what you are teaching. Some research indicates that boys especially can benefit from diagrams, semantic maps, and charts that may accompany a lesson. Even when children cannot read, they learn about the forms of recording through print by having ideas organized into schematic diagrams, key words written down, little pictures drawn quickly, and writing demonstrated.

You need to make this kind of visual display consistently, and to do that, you must have a place where children can easily see what is in front of them; however, you do not have to move from your central position in front of the students to write or draw. Many classrooms I have been in have calendars, visual aids, and charts in their teaching centres, but little space for spontaneous demonstrating in print or picture while the teacher talks.

It is also a good idea to make sure that there is chalkboard, whiteboard, or chart paper at a level where students can write words and letters, circle, or point. Although this doesn't happen in every lesson, these opportunities help students to learn and can help you monitor their understanding of the concepts presented. At the teaching centre you will also want to have an alphabet which is easily visible to the students and enough room to either hang or display any other needed visuals.

By the chart stand, which is often an easel because it allows for a firm back for writing, you may want to keep a can of permanent markers and a roll of white sticky tape, which is useful if something needs to be "erased" or covered. I make sure my chalk ledge has colored and regular chalk so I can use different colors to differentiate between things or organize semantic maps into categories using color.

For the students I like to have a set of cut-up small chalkboards handy and a box of sturdy sports socks, each with a piece of chalk inside. Every few months, I take the socks home to wash. Of course, small whiteboards and dry-erase pens are easy to use; you may want a small set of those for small-group work.

Involving All Students in Learning

When I began teaching many years ago, the common practice was for teachers to direct a question to the whole class and a number of students would put up their hands. The teacher would then choose one or two students to answer the question and go on to ask another question. This still happens today and is not necessarily a bad practice, but when one child answers, 20 or more children are not. Some of these children will be madly waving their hands, their faces full of frustrated annoyance when the teacher fails to call on them, and some will be completely tuned out.

To increase student involvement, it is helpful to provide opportunities for *all* students to answer the important questions that ensure students are thinking and learning. When you ask for a response from everyone or even half the children in the class, you are providing an environment where students know that they need to be listening and attentive, and are personally responsible for their learning. Receiving feedback about their correct thinking helps them see themselves as competent learners.

The effectiveness of partner work

One highly effective way to increase student involvement is to promote partner work.

Before you can get children to work in partners effectively, however, they need to be able to respond to your signals quickly.

I recommend teaching students signals at the beginning of the year. These may mean that they need to be quiet and look at you, stop what they are doing and freeze, clean up, start talking, stop talking, get into partners, come to the carpet, give an answer in unison, and put up their hands when they want to talk to you. My students and I spend a lot of time on these signals, making the practice of them a game. I compliment children who conform quickly.

Many teachers use many different words or devices or a combination of both to signal an expected behavior. For example, my colleague Janine uses a little metal frog "clicker" that means students need to stop and look at her. Its sound is pleasant and non-threatening, which a teacher's voice may not be! I have used the words *Eyes here* as a signal for students to stop, put hands in their laps, stop talking, face me, and give me eye contact. I say, "Partners!" to get them to sit knee to knee, eye to eye with their partners. Children love the game where I just say, "Partners!" and then "Eyes here!" and then "Partners!" again as they move quickly from being knee to knee with their partners to a "facing me" attentive position. Speeding this up usually ends in laughter, but sets the stage for them to know that partner time is about to stop and they will face me when I say, "Eyes here!"

Partners need to know if they are person 1 or person 2 in the partnership as you will often give directions for one partner to go first. Here's an example of how this works:

"When I say, 'Partners,' partner 1 will show partner 2 how to spell the word *with* on their chalkboards. Partner 2 will look at the word and give the word a big checkmark if they think it is right, or discuss with partner 1 how to fix it so it is right. 'Partners!'"

Then after a minute or so, I would say, "Eyes here!" They would all turn to look at me, and I would spell the word *with* on the chalkboard.

If you compare the above example to a situation where one child spells *with* on the board, you will see that when students work with partners, they will likely learn more effectively.

Another example of Partner Talk would be in a discussion. You might ask all the students to think of everything found in a sentence, give them a few ideas to prime their thinking, and then prompt them to put each item on a finger, saying it under their breath. Ideally, they would think of at least five things. When finished, each student makes a fist to keep all the ideas in the hand, and then partner 2 tells partner 1 all his or her ideas by unfolding a fist and touching each finger during the recount of ideas. Partner 1 tells partner 2 ideas in the same way. Students might think of letters, capitals, periods, spaces between words, ideas, orders, and facts, and in this way, each child is reviewing the content of the lesson as well as having opportunities to think "outside the box." Once students are in the *Eyes here* position, you can debrief by listing all their ideas on the board.

Again, compare this to a general question where hands are up and you get the same ideas on a list on the board, but without the involvement of as many students. During the partnering process, you can see who is having difficulty and can step in quickly to help, or make plans to do extra review with specific students.

Setting Appropriate Expectations

Jo Spies, the former Reading Recovery teacher leader in Vancouver, always told her in-service teachers that with some reading concepts, children didn't always "get it" the first time or sometimes even the second or the tenth time, but they would learn if we kept at it and sometimes changed our approach. The important thing was a little, not a lot and the consistency of every day — sometimes, it felt like building a sandcastle one grain of sand at a time!

Within this book, look for the lesson sections "Making It Simpler" and "Increasing the Challenge." The first section provides concrete ways to adapt lesson format or expectations to ensure that all students have achievable tasks; the second provides extensions for students who are above the expectations.

It is important that whatever expectations you have for a student can be met by the student. It is also essential that you *have* expectations for the student who is not learning as quickly as others. This struggling student is often the one to whom teachers say, "Just do your best!" and the child learns quickly that anything is good enough because teachers have low expectations and will accept attempts that don't reflect best work. To guard against that, set an achievable goal for the student, although it will be different than that of other children.

Unfortunately, there is no way you can protect such a student from knowing that the expectations for him or her are different from those of other students; however, if you often have different goals for both higher and lower achieving students, your students will readily accept that it is okay for students to do something different. For example, the goal of a lesson might be for students to learn to print their names on sheets of paper using manila tag card with their names written on it as models. For your struggling students, you might expect that they would write the first two letters of their names and write larger than other children do. Or perhaps you would expect the students to trace over the letters of their names, written on separate sheets of paper, starting at a green dot and ending with a red dot on each letter. For whatever task is given, the number of times it needs to be practised is given. When the task is finished, you may say: "You have done a great job of printing the first two letters of your name, and when I see these two letters I know that this work belongs to you. Good for you for working so hard. You are learning to write."

Many students have difficulties that go beyond knowing how to copy their names or print the letters of the alphabet — they are new language learners. These students have vast needs when they come to the classroom. In Kindergarten, *every* lesson is a language lesson where new concepts and vocabulary are practised and learned. It is important to ensure that English Language Learner

(ELL) students have opportunities to use the language orally as they practise and reflect on what they are learning about writing.

Ways to Assess Basic Skills

Assessment *for* learning, done before a lesson is taught
Assessment *as* learning, where teacher and students reflect on learning so far and determine next steps
Assessment *of* learning, based on specific criteria and using assessment tools

Assessment informs practice, so be careful about the assumptions you make about what children know. Many students come to school knowing how to identify letters of the alphabet and knowing many of the sounds that those letters make, but that doesn't mean they know how to isolate the sounds in a word, or that they can blend isolated sounds into words. Knowing rote answers to questions like, "What sound does a *B* make?" may be quite different from manipulating that letter and sound by answering, "What sound do you hear at the beginning of Barbara's name?" or "Use your /b/ sound to start a new word that rhymes with *slug*."

Although practice and exposure to basic skills to ensure mastery of a more subtle, but related skill set has value, it is inefficient to teach children what they already know. Much time on task is wasted by having students working on tasks that are much too easy for them. Having children circling the pictures of items whose words begin with an /s/ sound when they are already writing many words and sentences with /s/ sounds in them is a waste of time. It is always better practice to have students apply their phonetic abilities while writing ideas and facts — this dynamic phonics-in-action process ensures that students are working to the level of their own abilities.

Throughout the assessment process, keep in mind that students are motivated to learn through success and proof of their competence. Therefore, it is important to give students feedback about what they are doing right and the improvements they are making, and to mirror pleasure and pride in their accomplishments. In the regular lesson component "Reflecting on the Learning," there are questions that encourage students to look at their work and consider what they have learned, where they have done well, and sometimes, what goals they could set for the next day.

Some basic skills are easy to assess. A few ideas are outlined below.

Letters of the alphabet

Remember that although many of these basic skills related to writing conventions are important, they are never as important as ensuring that you are reading what children are thinking. The content of their writing should be the focus of your interventions about their writing.

Assessing what letters of the alphabet a child can identify is as easy as having a random list of letters and asking students to identify them. You might circle the letters they can identify in September in red, and then re-test in December and mark the new letters learned in green, to be followed up in April with another test, circling letters learned in yellow. An assessment list for letters, "Checking Alphabet Recognition," appears at the end of Chapter 2.

Spelling and use of conventions

At the beginning stages a good idea is to give a blank piece of paper, ask if the child can spell some words — any words — and then keep a record of words spelled. For example, you might say: "Can you spell your name, *Mom, Dad, no, yes*, or any color words?" For more proficient students, administer spelling tests, and for all students, look at their written work and make note of their use of spacing, size of letters, punctuation, ability to self-correct when editing, and so on. When you are making anecdotal notes about a child's writing, it is a good idea to include a comment or two about use of conventions. Numerous checklists and rubrics outline the specific criteria students need to meet to indicate they are able to use the Basic Tools. These descriptions can also form the basis of report card writing, and with a continuum of progress from "unable to do the task" to "demonstrates good ability that meets the age-appropriate standard," it is easy to see the progress over time.

Emergent learners, the focus of this book, have little or no practical experience, and so are dependent on direct instruction in some basic rules to help them proceed. Much of the assessment that teachers will do is seeing whether children are able to use these "rules" as they work. Much of the evidence of student progress is gathered by observing students' writing and making comparative notes between numerous writing samples in notebooks or portfolios. These samples should clearly indicate that students' use of writing conventions is improving over time.

Phonetic matches

In Kindergarten and early Grade 1, when students do not write an easily read text, keep a record of a child's story as it is given to you and underline the phonetic matches, so that both you and the parent who observes it can see that the student is making more phonetic matches as time goes on. An example is given below:

Phonetic matches are underlined.

Feb. 22 My mom and me are playing together & then I saw an airplane & my friend was inside the airplane & then we waved

Feb 24 One morning I woke up and then I see the clock was too late and then I will brush my teeth and go outside and walk to School.

Mar. 1 One day I see a rainbow and I love my mom and I think my mom love me to.

Mar 3 One day I see some flowers & a basket and I see a rainbow to [illegible] stars. nighttime I see some birds flying in the sky

March 10 - One day I walk and I walk then I see a rainbow bridge and beside the rainbow I saw a flower and basket.

Heather Gray, a retired Grade 1 teacher, recalls that her son could read before he began school and consequently missed out on a lot of phonetic instruction. Not until he was older did his parents discover that he had difficulty with spelling: he had missed some basic phonetic instruction that beginning readers usually get.

Keeping in Touch with the Home

When the home is involved with the school in many aspects of students' learning, it is often a recipe for success. Motivated students will be begging for pencil and paper to start writing on their own at home as well as in school. Teachers are wise to encourage parents to be comfortable with their children's explorations with print and to see that those explorations do not put pressure on the students.

Parents who express worry over teaching their children to print incorrectly need to be reassured that children will learn correct letter formation at school. Even if children are printing in only capitals or using different print forms than those taught at schools, their curiosity and interest are of primary importance. Nonetheless, it is a good idea to send home the two "Letter Formation" sheets (see Appendixes) so families know how the school would like letters made.

A typical Kindergarten and Grade 1 practice is to send newsletters or letters home on a regular basis to tell what students are learning at school. Many parents are concerned about spelling and would benefit from a clear explanation of how children's writing evolves over time and how invented spellings are part of the process that leads to standard spelling. A meeting with parents about early writing, where they can see the development of writing from first scribbles to legible print through examples or slides, is the best way to relate to parents.

It is hoped that some of the background information in each chapter here can be used to help teachers with explanations to parents of what children are learning and why.

Many primary teachers encourage children's writing by making a puppet or stuffed animal a class mascot and sending it home in a little backpack with a notebook where a student, with the help of a parent, can record through pictures or stories the adventures of the class mascot. This practice allows students and parents to work on writing skills together.

Keeping students' writing efforts during Writing Workshop in a notebook or collecting and putting them into a writing portfolio is valuable. When children write often, leafing through the notebook or portfolio helps to demonstrate student progress to a parent. Having the child's examples of independent writing should show progress in using more conventional ways of writing. It is important that student writing be dated and that checklists and anecdotal records be used often and shared with the parents, indicating both what skills you expect to see developed and how the child is faring with each of these skills.

At this juncture, scores are relatively meaningless. Parents want to know where their child is on the developmental continuum. They want to know what is expected, and they want to know how they can help. When parents ask, "How can I help at home?" try to make sure that the activities you suggest are fun and don't put undue pressure on the student. Suggest activities that have already been introduced to the student at school and that you know the student can do successfully. If possible, format the activity as a game that provides practice of a particular skill: that may make it appealing to both students and parents. Many of the fine motor skills and the phonetic ability of some children cannot be rushed and will develop slowly. Be sure to proceed slowly and carefully with parents who may be anxious about their child. Although some commercial workbooks have children practise printing and letter formation, I don't advocate workbooks in school — teachers have more interesting and effective ways to teach printing and letter recognition skills. However, workbooks can be useful for parents and students who want to practise these skills at home.

In the following chapters the essential skills that students need to know to become writers are outlined in anchor lessons and discussions of teaching during daily routines and play. Although teachers may want to add lessons that complement and support the ones provided here, these chapters outline a core curriculum of all the Basic Tools beginning writers need. These simple tools, such as the ability to print letters quickly and accurately and stretch out the sounds in a word one is trying to write, help students achieve a goal every teacher strives for: getting students to become independent writers as early as possible.

1

Putting Pencil to Paper

Many students come to school able to hold a pencil or felt pen correctly, to print their names in "school" script, and to draw recognizable pictures. These students are demonstrating at least one aspect of being ready for Kindergarten. However, some students do not have these skills so this chapter is for them: how to learn the very basic skills needed to put pencil to paper in such a way that good storytelling can unfold.

In this chapter there are three lessons: one on holding a pencil, one on writing one's name, and one on making simple pictures. These are anchor lessons and it is expected that you will add many more lessons to teach these concepts. The lessons have been designed so that you can differentiate the teaching to suit the range of learners that every classroom has: some very competent students and some whose lagging development in fine motor skills and other areas creates difficulties for them. For most students, the exposure to following directions and the opportunities for oral language are as important as the physical aspect of putting pencil to paper. Thoughtfully using the adaptations and extensions provided for each lesson will help ensure their suitability for all learners.

Here is how various students in Grade 1 printed their names in September of the school year.

How to Hold a Pencil Correctly

When my colleague Lisa is unsure about the "handedness" of a child, she plays a little game. She spills out small objects on the table in front of the child to see which hand he or she uses, although some may use both. Over time, though, a dominant hand for printing will usually surface. Only then does she encourage a child to use just one hand.

Knowing the dominant hand a child will use for writing is important. Since students do come to school without established hand dominance, it may be necessary to first observe what hand a child uses when picking up toys or using a spoon or fork in order to determine which hand is likely dominant. During the parent–child interviews that happen during the first weeks of Kindergarten, you can ask if the child is right or left handed. Children are now encouraged to use their dominant hand to hold a pencil. Many teachers find that children can hold a thick felt marker and chunky crayon or pencil much better than a standard pencil and recommend the use of fat crayons and thicker pencils for children's first attempts at writing. Most children can use a fat pencil adequately in Kindergarten, so the lessons here are tailored for pencil use.

EXPLORING THE PURPOSE

Although instruction in pencil grip is a primary purpose of this lesson, it has many secondary benefits for all students. Students will learn about following directions to the specific signals that their teacher wants them to focus on. They will learn the names of a number of different writing implements that they will use daily, and learn directional words, such as *top, bottom, left-hand side, right-hand side,* that help to orient them towards pencil-and-paper tasks.

GETTING READY

Paper sizes used in school copiers are usually talked about in terms of inches. Letter-sized paper is 8½ by 11, legal-sized paper is 8½ by 14, and the largest size of paper that goes into standard copiers is 11 by 17. Although Canada has in many instances adopted the metric system, these well-known measurements in inches are used here.

Before the lesson have paper for each child — preferably 11 by 17.

You will need fat paintbrushes, thin paintbrushes, fat felt markers, skinny felt pens, crayons, fat pencils, and sharpened standard pencils, as well as small bowls of paint and water cans for the paintbrushes.

Have a piece of drawing paper for you to model with, preferably on an easel or displayed on a chalkboard or whiteboard.

In addition to setting out materials, you could play a listening and watching game to help students get ready. With young children, gross motor movement is important both for cognitive development and for ensuring that they do not easily get distracted or restless. In this game, they move around the classroom using their whole bodies as they respond to directions.

You might ask students to touch the left wall, touch the ground (bottom), stop, reach for the ceiling (top), and touch the right wall. Between each direction, say "Stop!" as a signal for them to stop; then, ask them to respond to this question: "Where are we?" Doing so provides an opportunity for them to say the direction words out loud.

Vary the speed and tone of directions, sometimes whispering or using a loud voice, or giving the directions quickly or very slowly.

After the gross motor movement, say: "Now we are going to sit quietly at our desks or tables and play this game with our fingers on the paper. We are going to pretend that our fingers are our bodies and the paper is our classroom!" In this way, students' fingers go to the bottom, the top, the left side, and the right side.

HOW TO TEACH IT

It is easiest to teach this lesson to a small group of students around a table. Remember that students need to have had some experience with painting and play time with these materials before: the paints can be so tempting that it is hard for them to realize that they can't touch until the direction to do so is given. You might begin by telling them this:

"Today we are going to be learning about lots of things we can use to draw and write with. We are going to be using all these things to make special pictures. I am going to hold each thing up and I want you to tell me what it is."

Hold up a paintbrush, a crayon, a felt pen, and a pencil. Children name each item. Then, explain the game My Turn, Your Turn:

"I will show you how to use each one of these things, even though I know most of you already know how to use them. That will be my turn. Then, I will tell you what to do. That will be your turn. When your turn is finished, put the paintbrush, crayon, felt pen, or crayon back in the middle of the table, and wait for what I'm going to tell you to do next."

Emphasizing the movement top to bottom is helpful in preparing students for printing, where they will be making letters from top to bottom. This lesson establishes much of the language that students will use in writing and printing: top, bottom, left, right.

First, model where you want them to put their fingers, perhaps at the top of the page or at the bottom of the page, by placing a finger on your demonstration paper. Direct them to look at their paper. Children demonstrate by putting their fingers on the correct spots after each position has been modeled. Ask the children to say the names of the positions as they put their fingers in the right place: top, bottom, left, right.

After having determined that children know the positions top, bottom, left, and right on their paper, demonstrate how to hold the paintbrush. I lie the paintbrush across the palm of my hand, gripping it relatively close to the end between the thumb, forefinger, and middle finger.

Janine Reid, a literacy consultant, suggests that some children who have difficulty with pencil grip can be helped by placing a dime between their pinkie and ring fingers and then "pinching the pencil" with their other fingers.

"You use your thumb and two fingers to hold it like you are pinching it. It's best to hold it quite close to the end so you can control it. It's too hard to paint if you hold it up too high." Demonstrate.

"I'm going to dip it in the paint and wipe off the extra paint on the side of the bowl like this, and then I'm going to make two thick stripes going from the top to the bottom of the paper, starting on the top left side."

Ask the students to hold their paintbrushes, find the left-hand side, and paint the two stripes, finishing by putting their paintbrushes back into the middle of the table. Make sure that left-handed students have their paintbrushes in the right hand.

Lisa, my former teaching partner and an experienced Kindergarten and Grade 1 teacher, shared some of her best teaching ideas with me. Here is one example.

It is important to allow play time with materials before students are asked to work with them in a teacher-directed fashion. Once when attempting a math lesson using little cubes that can click together, Lisa found that her usually attentive students were ignoring her directions; instead, they got busy making long lines of linked blocks. When a resource teacher suggested that students play with the blocks first and then do the lesson, the lesson worked like a charm!

Next, direct students to another implement and give a demonstration of how to hold it and how many stripes to make. Use crayons, fat and skinny felt pens, and finally pencils. Emphasize the correct grip for each item, placing the tool between thumb and forefinger and holding it relatively close to the end for better control. Ensure that a child has an open web space — this means the thumb and forefinger form an oval when the child holds the pencil. Ask for the lines to go from top to bottom, working from left to right to make a striped picture. Be sure to follow a process that enables them to watch carefully as you demonstrate before they take their turn. If you vary the number of stripes and colors, the students will get practice at counting and following directions.

REFLECTING ON THE LEARNING

Find a time to talk to students individually about the work they have done and ask them the following questions to help them assess how well their learning went. Making sure that you tell them what they did correctly in this lesson is helpful for both building feelings of success and for labeling the learning that has taken place.

- Which line is your favorite?
- Which one is the straightest?
- Which of the things we used today was the easiest to use? Which was the hardest?
- Which one do you need more practice with?

It's important to label the learning that occurred. These specific comments on what students can do will make them confident learners:

"You can use all of these writing implements correctly by holding them the right way. You can make straight lines that go from the top of the page to the bottom of the page. How many lines did you make? Can you count them?"

You can reinforce the lesson by asking students to show you the thickest stripe, the stripe made with the skinny marker, the narrowest stripe, and so on. Doing this reinforces the language you want them to learn. Sometimes, you can do this with the whole group gathered together in order to save time.

NOTES ON ASSESSMENT

Before the Lesson: Do you know which children are left handed or don't have dominance over either hand? It's helpful to know who these children are and the information can be gathered from ways discussed in the introduction to this lesson. Some students have poor fine motor skills and may have difficulty with pencil grip. Have plastic pencil grips ready in case children need them in order to have sufficient control with their pencils.

During the Lesson: Most of the assessment is done through observations while the children are doing the task. You need to ascertain if the students hold the implements comfortably in the correct position and have control over a line made from the top of the page to the bottom.

It's important to observe the control that students have over their writing implements. Are the lines wobbly and not from top to bottom? Is this because of poor ability to follow directions or inability to hold the writing implement? Ask them to follow an instruction again and watch closely to see what the problem might be.

After the Lesson: This lesson also includes many language concepts that deal with comparison, for example the words *thickest, thinnest,* and *fattest.* Having students point to their thinnest or thickest stripe or count their stripes could also be used to monitor their understanding of some of the secondary learning outcomes of this activity.

MAKING IT SIMPLER

Make It Bigger: If the child has difficulty with fine motor skills, use a larger piece of paper placed on an easel or chalkboard and use only thick paintbrushes or felt pens to begin with. Or, have the child make stripes using chalk on a chalkboard or easel. As skills improve, make the paper size smaller and the writing implement finer.

Join the Stars: If a child has difficulty making a straight line or controlling the writing implement, place a tiny star at the top of the page and a star at the bottom of the page, and ask the child to make a line from the top star to the bottom star.

Use a Pencil Grip: Plastic pencil grips are available for students who have difficulty holding a pencil; or, if you don't have them available, a piece of modeling clay placed where the child would hold the pencil makes an appropriate "fatter" surface to hold on to. Some teachers have also wrapped masking tape around a skinny pencil to make a better grip for the student.

Develop Fine Motor Skills: If students have problems with pencil grasp, they can get better by stringing beads, using screwdrivers, picking up things with tweezers, and manipulating small objects.

The striped sheets the students produce can be used for an art project, for example, as background mats for cut-out pictures; covers of a book; or stripes cut horizontally to be used in a bulletin-board display. Melanie, a teacher colleague, did a "sunset" lesson by gluing a yellow sun on top near the centre or near the bottom.

INCREASING THE CHALLENGE

- Ask the students to use a paintbrush to make a thick stripe and then a thin stripe so that they can see how maneuvering the paintbrush in different ways can produce different thicknesses. The same can be done with felt pens.
- Vary the number of stripes so that students have practice with bigger numbers.
- Ask the students to demonstrate control of crayons and pencils by making wavy lines, zigzag lines, and so forth.

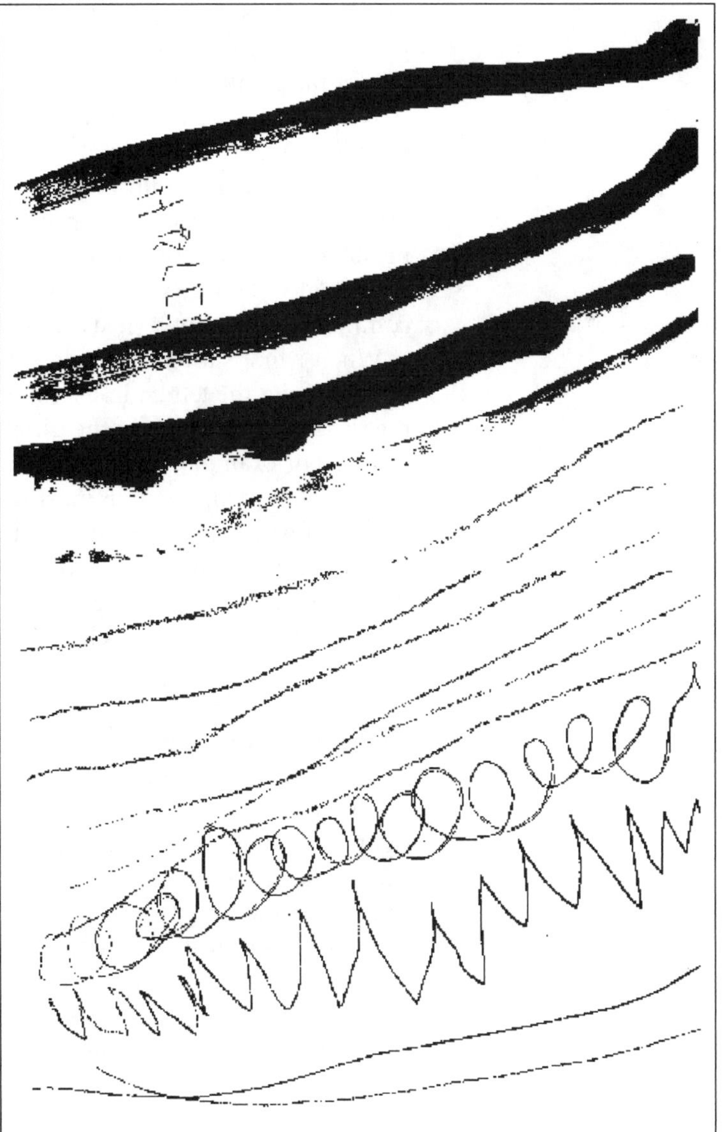

A student from Pleasant Valley Elementary School, Nanaimo, British Columbia, produced these stripes in blue in September of Kindergarten.

Printing Names

Children love learning to read or write their own names. When children come into their classroom and find their names by the cloakroom hooks where they hang their jackets, on the Welcome to Kindergarten sign the teacher has made, and on the table or place in the circle where they may be sitting, teachers have gone a long way in providing a welcoming place for students. Many teachers use a piece of manila tag to make a Name headband hat for each child that is then decorated the first day of school, or students have nametags that they wear around their necks on necklaces of string or name cards pinned to their shirts. Many of the songs that children first learn help every child learn the names of other children in their class. The classic song "The more we get together" is only one of many such songs that can be used to help students learn the names of their new friends quickly.

Many children will enter Kindergarten knowing how to write their names, often in capital, or uppercase, letters. Teachers will display the children's names printed in the traditional "school" style of a capital at the beginning of the name and then lowercase letters and expect that students will learn how to print their names in this "school" style over the course of the first few months. Even after a number of lessons on how to print their names, some children may be able to print only the first few letters of their names and may take several months to master the printing of their whole names.

Why teach a consistent style to all students? Why "school" style print for everyone? These are legitimate questions that parents and teachers may ask. The style of printing generally adopted in North American schools is made up of letters that contain circles, part circles, and straight vertical lines, and start with the pencil moving from the top of the letter to the bottom. I believe that the reason a consistent style is used is simply for ease of teaching, and the "school" style is a common manuscript style used in many schools.

When I first started teaching children to print in the early 1970s, we taught how to make the letters in a smooth top-to-bottom movement without taking the pencil off the page for the duration of the letter except to dot *i*'s or cross *t*'s and *f*'s. For example, the letter *a* was one smooth move of a pencil beginning at the top right going around, meeting the beginning of the circle and then immediately down; *b* and *d* went down and then traced the line up before it went around to make the ball part of the letter. By making each letter without lifting the pencil off the page, students learned to print quickly and there were no spaces between letter lines and circles. I still teach children to print like this.

EXPLORING THE PURPOSE

Students will learn more than just how to print their names during lessons where they make their names from a model the teacher provides. They learn how to follow specific teacher directions and learn where the top, bottom, left- and right-hand sides of a manila card or a page will be found. Printing their names from a model may be one of their first experiences of "copying" a model, but it will not be the last. Teaching students to observe carefully, to make the model letter or letters in the air with imaginary pencils or paintbrushes, and to note where to start and end letters is an important part of helping them develop the fine motor skills they need to print words. Stress that letters should be printed from top to bottom and where to start the printing.

Students who learn to print their names at home and come to school with their names printed in all capitals or with curved *t*'s and a's should not be told that the way they have learned to make their names is wrong or incorrect. Respectful teachers will assure students that they can read their names and are proud of them for learning how to write them; they will also say that names can be printed many ways.

It is important to accept the way that children print their names while also encouraging them to learn to print it in the "school" style that is used for the stories that children do in Kindergarten and Grade 1. A good way to demonstrate the variety of styles that can be used to print a name is to print the name of a classroom mascot or stuffed animal in many different fonts; students will see that the same name can look very different depending on how it is printed. An example of the name *Barney* is given below:

GETTING READY

It is a good idea not to provide erasers at this time. Children easily become dissatisfied with attempts and try to erase rather than starting over again. These erasures take time and can be very frustrating for both student and teacher. Erasing an attempt is less useful than continuing on and trying again.

- Print each child's name on a piece of a manila tag or cardstock, with the capital letter about 6 cm long (about 2 inches) and the other letters sized accordingly. (If you need to check how letters should be formed for school, see the alphabet charts in the Appendixes.) For beginning Kindergarten students, the name should not be on lines.
- For demonstration purposes, set on the board a large manila tag card with a simple four-letter name on it.
- Prepare the blackline master "Printing My Name" for each child and a larger copy on chart paper or chalkboard. (See page 35.)
- Provide a sharpened pencil for each child, either standard or wide.

In her classroom, Lisa makes sure that each of the children's names is printed on a manila tag card kept in a hanging pocket chart. To be more efficient, she has their first name printed on one side and the first and last name printed on the other. Students learn their first names and then progress to printing their first and last names together.

HOW TO TEACH IT

For the first lesson on teaching students how to print their names, I like to gather a group together at a table and play a My Turn, Your Turn game. I ask the students to watch while I trace over my sample word on the board with my pointer finger, making sure I emphasize the starting position and verbalizing as I go; for example, making a letter *a*, I might say, "I start at the top of where I am going to make my circle, go around to the left and then down." For a capital *D*, I might say, "First, I make a straight line down and then I go up to the top and make a nice curving line around to the bottom."

When students take their turn, tracing their names on their cards with their pointer fingers, I check to make sure that they are using their fingers to go from the top to the bottom and are systematically tracing letters from left to right.

When I next demonstrate making the name under the model with chalk or felt pen, I emphasize the little space that goes between each letter, while making sure they know the letters have to be close together without touching. Students may use the blackline master "Printing My Name" to print their names from the model on their manila tag cards.

This sample shows how one Kindergarten student printed his name in October of the school year. From Ladysmith Primary School, Ladysmith, British Columbia.

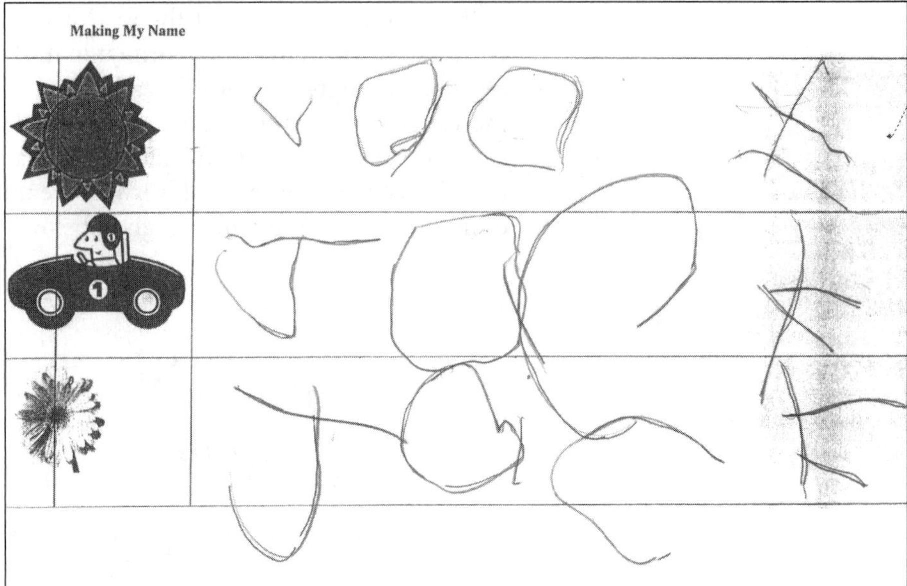

Here are more lesson ideas for helping students learn how to print their names.

Using buddies to help students print their names

Lisa has used her class of older buddies to do a fun activity that emphasizes the importance of printing names. After modeling the size and formation of the letters, she asks the big buddy to print the name of the younger child in huge chalk letters outside on the schoolyard pavement. The big buddy and little buddy walk single file through the correct path of each letter of the printed name. This can be done many times, with them taking turns as to who is the leader. They can use fingers to do the same thing and then make a "rainbow" name by tracing over the name on the pavement many times with different colors of chalk.

Putting names on a Yes/No graph

Printing names is so important that you will want to build this activity into the everyday routines that students follow. My colleague and daughter Kristine uses a Yes/No graph where there is a question at the top and places for students to "sign" their names under Yes or No. To begin, she uses very easy questions, such as "Is there an *a* in your name?" and she reads the question aloud so they can decide. This practice continues through the year, sometimes with the students writing their names on sticky notes posted on the graph (which means that the space around the graph does not get congested) and sometimes with individuals printing their names on the chart paper or whiteboard where the graph is.

The daily sign-in

Lisa provides a daily sign-in each morning. The children come into the classroom, hang up their coats and bags, and then sign in just like teachers do. There are 5 to 8 sign-in sheets and the students line up and sign any one of these sheets. They may use their manila tag card as a reference if they aren't exactly sure how to make their names. When the sheets are full of names, they become sheets for reading, which many students learn to read quite quickly. Later, mostly to save on paper, Lisa or her partner Melanie has the students use chalk and mini-chalkboards to sign in. Even simple routines, such as making sure that students sign their names on the board when they go to the washroom or to a specific learning centre, help provide practice in writing their names as well as monitoring where students are.

REFLECTING ON THE LEARNING

- Reflect out loud on the child's attempts and demonstrate your appreciation of the effort taken. You can say, "You have used the model of your name and made three names on this paper with your pencil." Or, if the child wasn't able to do three names, comment on what he or she has done: "This is the way we would like you to make your name at school. Which do you think is your best attempt?"
- Choose one or two letters that the child has done in good standard form and comment on how these letters are easy to read. "I can read this word easily. That's because you've made your letters the right shape and size." Comment on the top-to-bottom formation of letters.
- Collect all the student sheets and read the names out loud to the whole class so they can see that reading their names out loud is reading and can be done by anyone with the ability.

NOTES ON ASSESSMENT

Before the Lesson: Almost all students will benefit from this lesson even if they are printing their names in "school" print when they first come to school. They will be introduced to the procedures of following directions from a teacher model and will have the top-to-bottom movement in the formation of letters reinforced.

Asking students to print their names on a piece of artwork or letter home before you begin this task will allow you to see which students will need to be monitored closely and which students might need some adaptations to make the lesson more interesting for them.

During the Lesson: You will be required to observe both the students' ability to stay focused and follow directions in a timely fashion, and their ability to use a model to make their names during this lesson. Having a good pencil grip, control over fine motor movements, and ability to sustain concentration are all necessary to complete three tries of writing their names; you will be both assisting students to do this by pointing out where to start or where to continue and helping them form the letters with hand-over-hand trials of tracing their names on the model card.

Asking students to tell you what they have done so far will help them begin a process of self-assessment. You can ask: "Tell me about your job. What have you done so far? What do you need to do next? When will you be finished?" These questions will help students to maintain focus.

During this lesson you will be busy providing support for struggling students and so observations will need to be noted at a time after the lesson has been finished.

After the Lesson: If you collect the papers that students have worked on, you will be able to assess how well students were able to do this task during this first lesson. You will need to think back on their performance to determine whether focus and concentration were an issue, or if the main issue was an inability to copy a model with the fine motor skills needed. Be sure to make these observations in your anecdotal notes on the children in your class.

In the Appendixes, you will find a blackline master titled "Generic Assessment Checklist," which you may use to assess how well students can make their names. Below is an example of how you could rate students:

Assessing the basic skill of *Writing My Name*

Year *2007–2008*

1 unable to do the task
2 attempts the task with minimal ability
3 demonstrates average ability with distinct need for further practice
4 good ability—meets age-appropriate standards for the task
Description of proficiency levels, with 1 being the lowest and 4 being the highest

Date Assessed Names of Students	*9/09*									
Marie	*4*									
Gabriel	*1*									
Chandra	*3*									

MAKING IT SIMPLER

If children are unable to do this task, they will need some one-to-one assistance with an adult. Many of the ideas listed below will be helpful for children who have little control over their writing implements and do not remember how the letters of their names go. For each session with your students, try to find something that they were able to do reasonably well and give specific feedback on what they did correctly.

Green Dot, Red Dot: For students who need help with directionality, you can put a green dot on the beginning spot where the pencil should go to make the letter and then a red dot where the letter ends. Here are two examples:

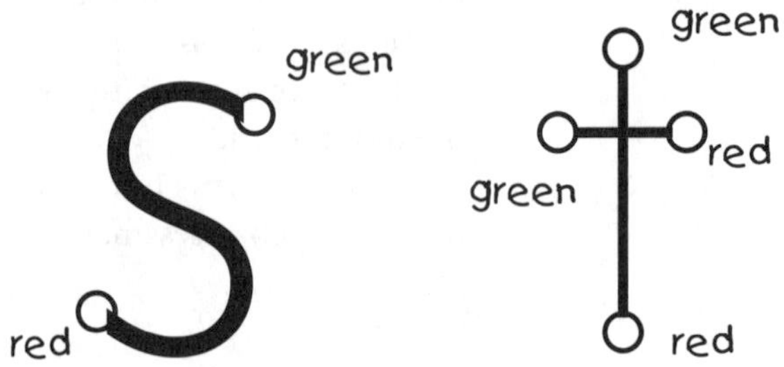

Trace the Letters from a Pencil: Sometimes, you may have to print the letters of names lightly and ask students to use skinny felt markers to trace them. Some teachers make names in small dotted lines that children can trace over.

Provide Tactile Stimulation: Ask students with fine motor difficulty to take their cards and make their names in a sandbox or in a long shallow box filled with salt, sand, or rice. Lisa uses a pie plate, which works well. Having their fingers trace letters through a substance helps to imprint the shape and direction of the letters in their names. Creating their names out of sandpaper letters and putting them on a card will also provide a tactile surface for students who need more sensory stimuli.

Limit the Goal: For example, telling students to focus on printing just the first two letters of their names may reassure them that you will always be able to recognize their names by these letters. Let them know that you will help them learn the rest of their names soon, but that they have made a great start.

Hand over Hand: If you can organize one-to-one time, have a student write his or her name on a chalkboard, hand over hand, with your hand over your student's to guide. As the student makes the letters, talk through it. It might sound something like this for the name Fay.

"We are going to make the capital *F* first, and we start at the top and make a straight line down, then we make a little line that goes from the top of the line we made to the right and then another little line halfway down that goes from the left to the right. We leave a spaghetti space, and then make an *a*, which is a circle and a line down. Finally, we make *y* which is a slanted line from top to bottom going from right to left, and then we make the top part a *v*."

You can do this with a felt pen or pencil. After a number of practices ask the student to print the name without help.

Use Magnetic Letters: To help students learn the sequence of letters in their names, print their names on the chalkboard, and ask them to use magnetic letters to make their names. Check to make sure that the letters are close together but not touching. Then rearrange the letters (I often say that a windstorm has come up and moved the letters around). See if students can make their names again.

Provide a Larger Surface: It may be helpful for students to print large-sized letters, using a surface such as a chalkboard or an easel, to get the movements and shapes of the letters more firmly entrenched in their minds. Many students have difficulty with the fine motor skills; they are better able to make larger arm movements on an easel or chalkboard. Gradually, they can move to smaller letters, first on the chalkboard or easel, and then on paper.

Position Paper for "Lefties": Left-handed students have difficulty visually monitoring printing since their hands cover their writing as they make letters from left to right, something that doesn't happen with right-handed students. It is helpful for them to position their paper so it is completely left of their midline. If you angle the paper so it lies parallel to the child's forearm, this can also help.

INCREASING THE CHALLENGE

- Have students make "rainbow" names once they have printed their names correctly on paper. Emphasize that the letters need to be big. They trace over their names with many different colors of crayons until they have a rainbow of colors.

- Provide modeling clay or play dough for students to make their names. They can make names over the models the first time and then underneath the models the second time. For making letters, it is helpful to show them all how to roll their play dough into "snakes": hold a small ball of play dough between the palms and rub back and forth, or roll the play dough between the surface of the table and the palm of the hands. These "snakes" work well to make letters.
- Let them use the magnetic board to find the magnetic letters to make their names and maybe the names of their friends.
- Have students paint their names with clean wet paintbrushes on the chalkboard and watch them slowly disappear.
- Prompt students to make their names two or three times out of random letters from a letter centre (see Chapter 3) with many letters created from sources such as Scrabble tiles and letters cut out of wallpaper or colored paper.

Here are examples of how Spencer, Janae, and Nicholas, Kindergarten students at Pleasant Valley Elementary School, Nanaimo, British Columbia, printed their names in September.

Making Simple Pictures

The purpose of these lessons is not to show any "right" way to draw, and teachers should be careful not to make a comment such as, "That's not the way I showed you to make a person." Drawing is always a personal, creative act. Our job as teachers is to acknowledge that respectfully, while occasionally encouraging students to extend their drawings by adding detail.

When students are first asked to make stories in a Kindergarten classroom, the teacher expects that they will make drawings to represent part of what they wish to say, and then the teacher will listen as the student tells the stories illustrated by their pictures. For some students, this may be a word or two; for other students, it will be a detailed number of sentences that describe a major event. For all students, however, there is a need to be able to graphically represent some objects that will illustrate the storytelling. Some students may not have any experience with drawing and are able to do only scribbles. It is helpful for students to know how to make simple pictures; doing a "directed drawing" activity is one way in which students will learn how to draw recognizable objects and experience the pleasure that drawing competence can bring.

EXPLORING THE PURPOSE

Teaching this lesson will help students develop confidence in their ability to graphically produce a picture that tells a story. They learn the "shape" words and learn to follow directions. They also learn the importance of details in drawings and are ready to include them in drawings asked for in Writing Workshop and other activities.

GETTING READY

I have chosen this lesson on drawing a person because young children, naturally egocentric, tell stories mostly about themselves! Being able to represent a person is very practical for storytelling.

Have a writing implement and either a large piece of chart paper ready or a space on a whiteboard or chalkboard easily visible to the students in the group. It is also helpful to have a visual chart that shows the basic shapes of circle, square, oval, rectangle, and triangle available for students so that they will have a reference for making these shapes. The students each need a piece of paper and a pencil, crayon, or skinny marker for drawing.

Before you begin this lesson, it is helpful to review the essential shapes that will be needed in these drawings: oval, circle, square, rectangle, and triangle, describing each one. (It is not necessary for children to be able to recognize and name these shapes to do this lesson, but the review is helpful.)

HOW TO TEACH IT

Since this is directed drawing, you would usually start with a shape and describe how it is made as you make it large on a piece of chart paper. You then ask students to do the same thing on their chart paper:

My colleague Heather has a way to help students position shapes correctly. She has students fold their paper into four quadrants and then she demonstrates where to put their pencils by pointing to the place on her paper or on the board and saying things like "We will make the oval shape a bit above the centre fold, and our shape will hug the fold line that stretches from the top of the paper to the bottom."

"We are going to start with an oval shape and we will do a My Turn, Your Turn lesson. Watch what I do with my felt pen. I want to make my shape near the top of my page and leave some room at the top and lots more at the bottom. I start at the top of the shape and then stretch to the left a little bit and then I go down, not all the way to the bottom, and make an oval shape just like an egg. I come back up and loop right to where I started."

Then, ask the students to find their place on the paper where they will begin and either make the same shape with their pencils or use their fingers for a "practice run." In this kind of lesson, beginnings are the hard part so spend some time checking to make sure that everyone has been able to make an oval in the centre of a page before continuing.

Explain what you are going to draw today. You might tell them: "Today we are going to make a funny person with this shape. I will make one thing and then it will be your turn." Add a neck, describing the motions: "I am going to make a little square at the bottom of the oval that will be the neck; now you make a neck."

It is always helpful to talk about what you are doing while making shapes or letters. Doing so provides students with both the visual and the auditory stimuli to help them make the shapes. Including phrases such as "just like an egg" or "around the lake" helps them make pictures in their minds.

Continue like this with a circle for a head, a square body, and then rectangle arms one by one, and rectangle legs one by one; then, add details, such as hair, ears, facial features, buttons on a shirt, belt, fingers and shoes, depending on how capable your young artists are and how detailed you want the figure to be. Add only one feature at a time, asking students to watch as you describe each movement and name each shape; then, ask students to take their turn.

To complete the picture you might want to get the students to consider where this person is, and ask what kinds of details they can add so that you will know if they are on a sidewalk or in a yard. You might also suggest that they give some details about the weather or the kinds of things they will be using to have fun or do some work. In this way you can prompt them to think of the story that might accompany this picture. Encourage them to use a number of different colored crayons to make their pictures colorful.

Using a sideways oval, you can make a fish during a different lesson. You may want to make your oval by describing your journey as "walking around the lake." Add a triangle tail fin, some triangle side fins, a mouth, and a round eye. Add scales as well if you like. Use the same method of adding only one feature at a time on your copy and then ask the students to take their turn. This could be done in the same lesson if students are attentive or may be done in another lesson.

You may find that only one drawing per lesson can be done in the 15 minutes allotted, but let children have several lessons creating different objects so they will have many opportunities for practice.

This lesson can be repeated using a square as a central figure to make a house or a car, a rectangle to make an apartment building and a truck, and a circle to make a sun and a flower. The simple progression of figures is shown below:

Two Progressive Drawings

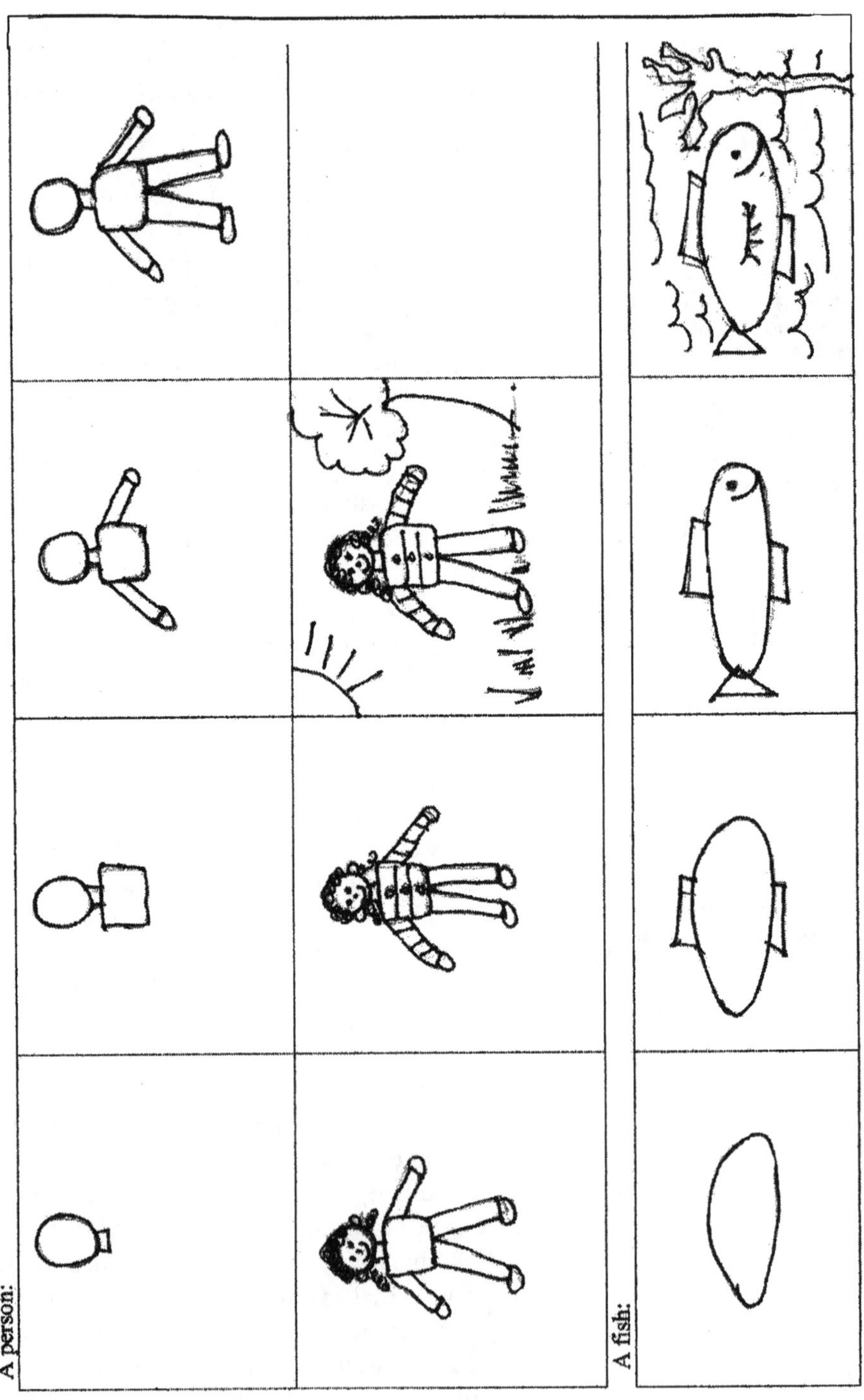

REFLECTING ON THE LEARNING

Students can benefit from the teacher reflecting out loud on children's pictures, making comments such as these:

"When I look at this figure, I see a happy person with a big smile, big green buttons on his shirt, rather short rectangular legs, and curly brown hair. I know a lot about this person you made because you drew so many details. Can you tell me what you like about your person?"

To help students with the concept of drawing in order to tell a story, ask them if they can think of a story about this person. What might this person do?

Students need to recognize that drawings are often made from the simple shapes reviewed at the beginning of the lesson. Check to see if they can name the shapes they used in the pictures they have drawn.

NOTES ON ASSESSMENT

Before the Lesson: Students will need to have a reasonable pencil grip to do these drawings. A good assessment of whether students will be able to draw the person would be to get them to draw a circle, a rectangle, and a square after you have drawn the shapes on the board; if they can do a reasonable job, they should be able to do this lesson.

Another good idea is to ask them to draw a person on a piece of paper before you do the lesson. They can then compare their first drawings to the second drawings. It is hoped they will find that they included numerous details in the second pictures that they didn't have in their first.

During the Lesson: This activity can be used as a tool to determine who has difficulty with following specific directions or creating basic shapes. You can also see quite quickly which students can detail small features, like buttons and eyebrows. Seeing what environmental details surround the person can help you determine their facility with adding details that tell a story. Most students will be able to attempt it, but if students are getting frustrated during this lesson, let them stop and finish on their own, commenting on their good beginnings. Some students will lack the focus to be able to maintain the considerable attention needed to complete this task.

To help students use assessment as part of their learning, ask: "Did this lesson help you to draw people better?" "What did you do for the first time in this lesson?" Accept their responses, asking them to tell you how it helped or why it didn't help, if they can.

If students were unable to do most of this lesson, it is helpful to provide some individual time with a side-by-side model provided by you or another adult, such as a teacher aide or parent volunteer. Providing this assistance will help the student feel more successful and gain practice for fine motor skills. Sometimes, it is not immediately clear why students cannot do this activity. Perhaps they have difficulty focusing and following directions one step at a time. Perhaps frustration with making a mistake keeps them from going on to the next step. Sometimes, it is just poor control over their fine motor skills. To ascertain where the student needs help, you will need to pay close attention to where the task falls apart for the student and what strategies you may employ to help.

After the Lesson: The questions below will help you assess student ability to create a simple picture by following the directions of a structured lesson. It is helpful to later ask the student to draw a person independently and see if he or she has included the details from this lesson.

1. Was the student able to make an oval shape, a square shape, a rectangular shape?
2. How many details did the student manage to add? Just a few? Many?
3. Was the student able to systematically follow directions?
4. How much control over fine motor skills was there?

MAKING IT SIMPLER

Have Modified, but Definite Expectations: This exercise is a good way of assessing to see how much fine motor control students have or if they have the attention span and focus to follow directions. If they don't, you need to adapt the lesson as you go. You could ask these students to do some of the big shapes, but not ask them to draw some of the more difficult details, such as the scales on the fish or the chimney on the house. Invite them to add what they like to basic four-step pictures and to color their pictures. Do remember to ask for the big shapes, and comment on their ability to follow the few simple directions you have given.

Provide a Shape Already Drawn: In this lesson on drawing a person, it might be helpful to have the oval head and the body square already drawn on the paper and then invite students to add the details. Although you want to have children doing as much as possible by themselves, having some shapes made for them will ensure that their product will be recognizable and look like a person, fish, house, or whatever. This will give the students some satisfaction in making a recognizable object. In the Kindergarten sample at the bottom of page 33, the oval for the head was given to the student before the lesson began.

Create a Group for an Easier Lesson: Identify a few students who had difficulty with the drawing lesson as it was given and group them together for a lesson on one of the easiest drawings, for example, drawing a sun, an apple, or a tree. This can be followed up by other lessons that focus on a particular simple object. These tasks will help students get accustomed to the language of directions and feel success in making recognizable pictures. After sufficient practice (over a few weeks) with smaller, less detailed pictures, have them draw the human figure again. Save their first attempts so they can compare their work — comment on how much they have learned!

Larger and Thicker: Some students benefit from making larger shapes on larger sheets of paper and doing it with thick felt pens or crayons rather than pencils, where they have more control over their drawing. They could also work side by side on a chalkboard, where they can make bigger shapes and have an easy writing implement (chalk) to use.

INCREASING THE CHALLENGE

- This exercise is suitable for everyone, even adults, but more capable artists will find that the figure is not very lifelike. You may want to suggest that they next make the basic shapes lightly with pencil and then use a darker crayon or felt pen over their fainter pencil shapes to make bodies with a waist and legs shaped more accurately.
- Ask students to provide even more details than what you have asked for and to be ready to explain what they are; to use what they know of "patterns" in their coloring; or to provide other details that help tell a story.

This simple picture was drawn by a student at Ladysmith Primary School, Ladysmith, British Columbia, in October of Grade 1.

In this Kindergarten student sketch from Pleasant Valley Elementary School, Nanaimo, British Columbia, the oval for the head was provided. The drawing was done in September.

This student sample from Pleasant Valley Elementary School, Nanaimo, British Columbia, comes from September of Grade 1.

Here is another student sample from Pleasant Valley Elementary School, Nanaimo, British Columbia. Note the greater detail in the setting.

Printing My Name

Assessment Checklist for Putting Pencil to Paper — The Early Basics

1 unable to do the task
2 attempts the task with minimal ability
3 demonstrates average ability with need for further practice
4 demonstrates good ability that meets the age-appropriate standard for the task

Pencil Grip

Dates:						*Comments:*
Holds pencil in proper position with open web space between thumb and forefinger						
Pressure on paper is not too heavy or light						
Able to draw a relatively straight vertical line from top to bottom of page						
Able to grip correctly a variety of writing implements and draw straight lines						
Able to control directionality in pencil control as in moving dot to dot						

Printing Names

Dates:						*Comments:*
Can copy name if given a model						
Can print whole name with correct letter formation						
Can write own name without looking at a reference						
Can recognize and read own name in numerous settings						

Drawing Simple Pictures

Dates:						*Comments:*
Is able to do a 3-step directed drawing						
Is able to do a 5-step directed drawing						
Is able to do a 9-step directed drawing						
Is able to add appropriate details to a directed drawing						

2

Identifying and Making Letters of the Alphabet

Learning to read and write are processes that present challenges to teachers and students alike. This chapter addresses how to teach students to identify and create the smallest units of this process: each letter of the alphabet. Later, in Chapter 4, the focus is on phonemes, or the sounds that the letters of the alphabet make, but here the major focus is on the naming and correct formation of letters that make up the alphabet.

In this chapter, teaching ideas that will help students remember the shapes of letters as they learn to make them accurately are presented. There are also some little stories and chants that help students match letter name, sound, and shape. You will also find an alphabet rap, or chant, that matches the alphabet stories that teach students how to identify and make the letters of the alphabet. Some suggestions on how to use alphabet books in your classroom are also included. A list of recommended alphabet books is provided.

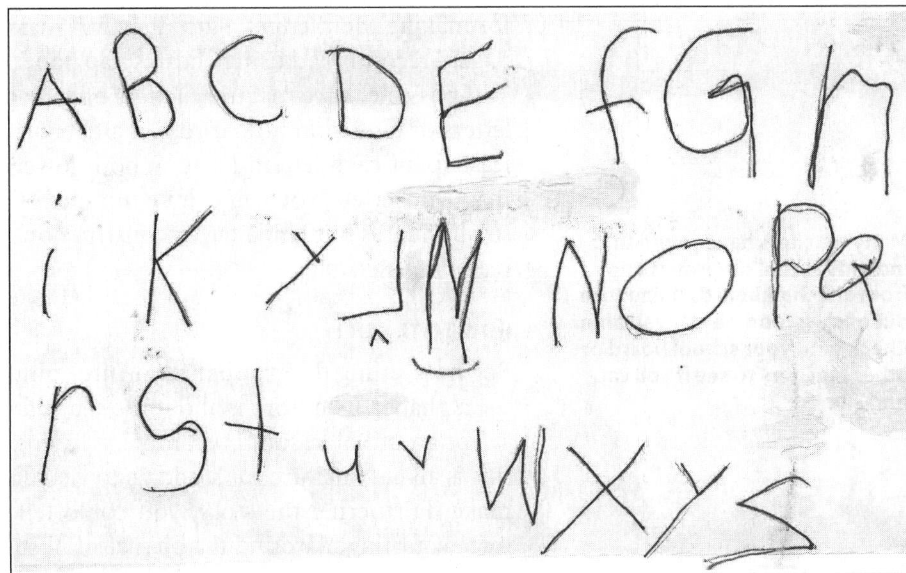

These letters of the alphabet were printed by a primary student named Seth.

Alphabet Stories

At the end of this chapter, you will find "Consonant Stories" and "Vowel Stories." The brief stories that they provide can be used to teach a similar lesson with any other two or even three alphabet letters that look different from one another.

There are so many resources and ways to teach letters of the alphabet and all of them work! Using alphabet stories is just one that is effective. The use of stories is an excellent teaching tool which makes those syntactic connections come alive in a student who needs help in matching the shapes and names of letters. Teaching a lesson using two letters that are varied in shape is a good way to start.

EXPLORING THE PURPOSE

Students need to be able to recognize letters of the alphabet and make them correctly. For students to be able to print quickly, it is helpful for them to start at the top and then go to the bottom of a letter; establishing this pattern early will help to ensure that the students won't develop habits that are hard to break. How do students remember what a *C* looks like when they are given its name? One helpful way to remember is to know that *C* is "a cookie with a bite out of it." By relating the word *cookie* to both the picture of a *C* and the sound at the beginning of *cookie*, shape, sound, and name of letter are incorporated into one simple story. Since most students can remember stories easier than symbols, teaching a story helps trigger a visual picture that corresponds to the letter *C*.

When students learn to read, they need to not only identify letters in words and match phonemes with those letter shapes, but do it quickly. Fast responding is an often overlooked, but important skill in both reading and writing. The goal is for students to make letters quickly, with automaticity, or without the need to think about the shape. Although neatness is important too, and quickly made letters may not be made as accurately as letters that have been carefully drafted, experience proves that teaching fast responding is more important.

GETTING READY

Make sure that you have a good-sized space on your chalkboard for demonstrating how to form letters. If you lack a chalkboard, have a large piece of chart paper ready. The students will need either individual chalkboards or paper and pencil for making their letters. Since they will make many letters which will easily fill a page, I recommend using cheap scrap paper rather than notebook pages.

If possible, have magnetic letters on a magnetic board or a number of cut-out letters or letters on little cards on a flat surface for students. There should be at least six of each letter: *T* and *S*, both lowercase and capitals. If you don't have magnetic letters, you can print a number of capital and lowercase *T*'s and *S*'s on small squares of manila tag or construction paper (5 cm square), and have them ready in an envelope.

Many teachers have found that individual chalkboards cut up from old chalkboards being torn out of classrooms are invaluable. Check with your school board or other teachers to see if you can find some.

HOW TO TEACH IT

Begin by telling the group that you are going to share a story about two letters of the alphabet. The story is about the shape and sound that each makes.

For an initial lesson, I recommend saying, "*S* is a snake that says *ssss*" because this is an easy picture for students to visualize, although not the easiest shape to make. Furthering the story, you could tell more about the snake's shape and trace your finger around the picture of it, starting at the head.

Don't expect children to be exact in sizes of letters, but they should know that capitals are big and most lowercase letters are half the size of capitals. I have often described tall lowercase letters, such as *f, t, p, b,* and *d*, as teenagers in the letter family. Like all children, they are still "little," but they are as tall as their parents, the capital letters. This analogy helps students distinguish between capital and lowercase letters. It is best for them to be able to do this at the beginning of their writing practice.

"He likes to lie in the sun and his body follows a path that goes to the left and then around the rock, and loops around the next rock, which is just under the first one. We say the *s* goes around the rock and around the rock. The rocks in this picture are imaginary, but they would look like little dots one on top of another."

You could put little dots where the rocks would be and make the *s* around them, saying: "When we make a capital *S* it is big, and when we make a lowercase *s*, it is about half the size."

It is helpful to have students make the *S* large in the air with their pointer fingers first. Encourage them to verbalize while they make the *S*, as speaking aloud helps them remember where to start and how to proceed. "*S* goes around the rock and around the rock."

Make the letter on the board as students trace it in the air and on their partners' backs and on their hands. Then ask them to make it on their chalkboards very big, and then smaller, slowly first until they have the feel of the shape, and then quickly. Have them practise making lots of big *S*'s and smaller *s*'s. Since a common confusion for *S* is to begin making the letter at the left, stress starting where the snake's head is, at the right, and following the body around the rock and around the rock.

Next, introduce another letter — *T* is a good choice. The story for *T* might be "*T* is a table for two for tea." Show them where the cups go and explain that the lowercase *t* looks different as you describe and demonstrate how it is made. Sometimes, while pointing to the part of the *t* above the horizontal line, you might tell them this:

"It is still a table for two for tea, but on this table you have a place to hang the menu which tells you that you can buy a piece of cake or cookie with your tea."

If you teach in an area where there are still telephone poles, you can create another great visual picture story for *t*.

Follow the same process used for *S* with *T*, having students make it in the air, make it on partners' backs, and make it with their fingers on the chalkboard before they start writing it. Emphasize the top-to-bottom line first and then the left-to-right line to either make a capital *T* or lowercase *t*. Make sure that students have practice verbalizing how the letter is made "straight down and a table top" or "straight down and a telephone pole." They should recognize that each person needs enough space for a teacup so the top line should be centred on the bottom line.

To provide practice in quick recognition of the shapes of the letters, you may use the magnetic letters and show them how to quickly sort all the *t*'s and *s*'s into two groups, and then scramble them — I usually suggest that an imaginary windstorm has come up. Then, ask them to group the letters again. (However, this is an individual game; it may be difficult for every child to have a turn with the magnetic letters.)

A reproducible page, "Vowel Stories," allows students to focus on vowels and add images that relate to the text. See page 54.

To provide individual practice, print the letters on paper squares and have children practise grouping them quickly. You could also have them glue letters into two separate groups after much practice separating them quickly into two piles of *T*'s and *S*'s. Provide many opportunities for them to say, "*S* is a snake" and "*T* is a table for two for tea," so that these stories will stay with them.

Consonant Stories

Here are some of the consonant stories I have used with young children. The stories — simple sentences that relate how to make the letter — may help students who think visually to remember how to make various letters. For example, the letter *b* could be shown as a baseball bat at the left and ball attached to it bottom right, the letter *h* could be shown as a figure sitting on the curved part of the letter with a speech bubble saying, "ha, ha," the letter *v* could be turned into a heart to represent a valentine, and the letter *x* could be shown with eyes in the top portion. Note that each story includes words that begin with the focus letter. You may of course devise your own.

b is a bat and ball.
c is a cookie with a bite out of it.
d drags a drum.
f is a fireman with his hose.
g is a guppy with a long tail.
h is ha ha happy to be sitting down.
j is a jumping jack with a big nose.
k is a boy ready to kick a can.
l is a lady tall and straight.
m is a set of mountains.
n is a nose with nostrils.
p is a pan with a handle you can hold.
q is a quiet queen.
r is a rooster.
s is a snake.
t is a table for two for tea.
v is a valentine.
w is a weird bird with wings.
x is it.
y is two talking heads going yackety-yak.
z is a zipper.

REFLECTING ON THE LEARNING

Asking the questions below can help you determine if students benefited from the lesson; it will also give you an opportunity to reinforce the names, shapes, and ways of making the letters.

- Tell me about the letters you made. Can you read them to me?
- Do you know the story you can say when you make *S*? (*S* goes around the rock and around the rock.) What is the story for T? Can you tell it to me?
- Find an *S* that the student has made correctly and say, "You have made this *S* correctly; it has two loops that go the right way: around the rock and around the rock." Do the same for *T*, commenting on how straight the line is, how the top part is centred on the line below. By doing this you are reinforcing the criteria for making the letters correctly.

NOTES ON ASSESSMENT

Before the Lesson: It is helpful to know how many students can identify random letters in the alphabet before you begin a unit of study on alphabet recognition. Many students may recognize the names of letters of the alphabet, but may not know how to print them accurately and so that needs to be assessed as well. You can assess letter recognition by giving students a chance to identify random uppercase and lowercase letters as you point to them. At the end of this chapter is "Alphabet Recognition Chart," which you can use for assessment purposes.

To assess what students already know about making letters of the alphabet, ask them to make them for you quickly without looking at an alphabet chart. You would just say, "Make me *s, a, t, p, w.*" It is better to do this with random letters than with letters in the proper alphabetical order. If you find that most of your students know the names of the letters of the alphabet, it is advisable not to spend too much time in formal lessons on letter names. What you may find is that there are groups of letters that some children find confusing, perhaps *b* and *d*, or *p* and *q*, and spending time on these letters will benefit everyone. Many more children will not make the letters correctly and will need lessons on printing the letters quickly.

During the Lesson: Give children a random group of eight letters by printing them on a sheet, or create a group of random magnetic letters and ask them to find an *S* and a *T* and see if they can differentiate that shape from the others.

Ask students to make a capital and lowercase *T* and *S* on a piece of paper while you check to see if they start at the top and use the right directions. At this time do not expect to see accurate dimensions, but to see that the lowercase *s* is smaller than the capital, and that letters start at the top and go to the bottom.

Parents often become concerned about students who make reversals such as *d* for *b* or backward *z*'s or *s*'s. Very common in Kindergarten and Grade 1, these reversals don't necessarily mean that students have a learning disability. If they persist into Grade 2 or 3, though, they may indicate some difficulty with visual perception.

After the Lesson: Since students will be making these letters many times again and this may be a first exposure to making them, I wouldn't yet do a formal assessment of letter knowledge or formation. However, note who is having difficulty so that you can better assess what that child's particular difficulties might be.

At the end of this chapter, there is the checklist "Assessment Checklist for Recognizing the Alphabet," as well as the related chart "Checking Alphabet Recognition." These can be used to formally assess whether students know letter names. You can also ask students to print the names of all the alphabet letters in order and note any letters that might be reversed, missed, or made incorrectly.

MAKING IT SIMPLER

Do One Letter, Not Two: Plan only one letter per lesson, and when it is time to group letters, have students find just the *s*'s or just the *t*'s to group together out of a range of random letters. You could do this if you have limited time or have many students who lack information on how to make the letters correctly.

Here is a good trick for helping students remember the correct formation for *b* and *d:* get them to make their hands into fists with their thumbs pointing upward, put their knuckles together, and tell them the picture made with their hands represents the word *bed*, with the *b* being the headboard and the *d* the end. In this way students can check their printing to see if they have made *b* or *d*.

Hand over Hand: If students are having difficulty making the letter on their chalkboards or papers, put your hand over theirs to guide them in the direction and shape of the letter. As you do the letter together, have them say the story with you. Then, ask them to try it on their own.

Create a Dotted Line Model: Have students trace over a number of letters made with dotted broken line or trace over light pencil-drawn letters you have made. Then, ask them to try printing on their own.

Highlighted Letters: A suggestion from Terrill, a Grade 1 teacher in Ladysmith, British Columbia, is to have students trace over penciled letters or their names on a model you have provided with a highlighter.

Make It Bigger: Ask students with fine motor difficulty to make a letter on the board with chalk or with a thick felt pen on a large piece of paper.

INCREASING THE CHALLENGE

- Have students make patterns using *S*'s and *T*'s in brightly colored crayons around the edges of a piece of drawing paper. In the middle, they can make pictures of snakes and tables for tea that tell a story.
- Invite students to find objects around the room whose names begin with *S* or *T* and to draw them in little booklets or, if labeled, print the words under a column labeled *S* or *T*.

Kindergarten students from Pleasant Valley Elementary School, Nanaimo, British Columbia, produced these printing samples of the letters *t* and *s* in September of the school year.

Six Alphabet Stations

Many early primary classrooms adopt a stations approach to teach a particular unit of study. In this approach, students have hands-on experiences at a table or other part of the room where a specific activity to reinforce or teach the skill is provided. By creating stations the teacher ensures that the unit of study provides many different ways for students to become familiar with their subject. Unlike a learning centre, a station is usually temporary, set up for just a week or two; a learning centre is usually kept for a longer time, often the whole year.

At each station, children are given directions about what to do and a specified time, in this instance about 10 minutes, to perform each task. When they have completed the task at one station, they are then asked to go to another station and do a different task. Sometimes, the directions and demonstrations of what to do for each activity are given by the teacher to the whole class; at other times, a teacher, older buddy, or teacher aide at the station provides directions and assistance. The students are divided up into as many teams as there are stations and move from station to station with the members of their team.

The six stations described below should provide some excellent "play" while students learn the alphabet. You may have students complete two stations a day and then have the stations set up for two more days until all students have had a turn at all stations, or choose some other arrangement that works well with your allotted time. For young students who learn by doing tasks, these experiences provide opportunities to engage all their senses in learning new concepts. The letters of the alphabet are a major part of the learning curricula for beginning writers, and what is described in the pages that follow is a multi-sensory, creative way for students to explore those letters.

EXPLORING THE PURPOSE

Although some students learn the letters of the alphabet readily, other students need many and varied exposures. By working at these stations, students have many opportunities to see, hear the name and sound of each letter of the alphabet, and most important of all, make the letters of the alphabet using different kinds of media with various textures and visual differences. Students will be seeing these letters not just in the normal on-a-line way, but isolated from others, upside down, and on their sides. These exploring activities are not only fun, but allow students to become thoroughly familiar with the shape, look, and feel of each letter, something that needs to be learned in order to read and write. You may choose to create stations for each letter of the alphabet or for just those letters that many of your students struggle to make or identify. These station tasks are especially useful for such letters as *b*, *d*, *p*, and *q* which can be quite confusing — students need lots of exposure to get the balls and circles in the right places. The order you choose is not too important, although it makes sense to start with easier-to-make letters first, and then go to more complex letters.

You may want to use a storage unit of small plastic boxes, usually holding craft supplies or nails and screws, for an Alphabet storage box. Each of the 26 or more boxes has the letter on a label on the front of the box, and in each box are small items whose names begin with that letter. These items can be used all year long for many different alphabet games. My colleague Heather uses empty plastic containers with lids that have the name of the letter on the lid and keeps these containers in a special box. The larger containers hold larger objects and more of them!

GETTING READY

A few days before implementing stations, announce that the class is going to celebrate the specific alphabet letter. Send home notes to parents asking for help in finding small inexpensive objects or magazine pictures of things whose names begin with that letter. You may first want to show students a number of items, such as plastic models of animals and a toy cup or camera. Suggest that the kitchen and toy box are good places to search for items and that children and parents could do this activity together. Provide a few days for each child to bring in an item. Students who do not bring something from home may find objects whose names begin with that letter in the classroom. I often have items available for students who forget to bring any from home.

HOW TO TEACH IT

At the carpet

When students bring in all their objects, which are displayed on a table, invite them to play an I Spy game and as each object is guessed, write the name of the object on the board, commenting on how the word begins with the focus letter, for example, *C*. You may want to do this for 5 to 7 items, and then ask individual students to come up, find all the *c*'s, and circle them. Perhaps two or three students can come up and circle the letter *c* anywhere it appears in a word.

The students can later use the objects for an I Spy game of their own or at a special "I Spy" centre during playtime.

Station 1: Making a picture out of the focus letter

At a table set out felt pens, crayons, and possibly other media, such as sparkles and paints, depending on the time allotted for this task. Provide a stack of drawing paper on which you have drawn the focus letter of the day in large size.

You could brainstorm some ideas and give some sample pictures to help students decide what scene the focus letter could be part of. Invite them to turn the paper upside down or on its side. In this way, if the focus letter is *C*, students could view the letter as the collar of a dress for a beautiful princess, a horseshoe pit, the back of someone's head, or a floating device in a pool full of swimmers. It is helpful to have students notice that if you turn a *C* on its side it looks somewhat like a letter *u*.

Students add to their *C* pages with crayons and felt markers to make beautiful pictures that clearly indicate what the *C* is. They should aim to add lots of detail and use all the space. They could make a story at the bottom saying, "My *C* is a __________."

Station 2: Finding the focus letter in our names

For this you need duplicated sheets featuring the names of everyone in the class.

Students are given three tasks at this station. One is to circle all the instances of the focus letter — for example, *C* — that they can find; another is to count them; and the third is to print the names of the children whose names have a *C* in them. Adding the task of printing names provides practice and makes sure that everyone is busy for the allotted 10 minute time.

Station 3: Making the focus letter into a cookie

If you don't want to fuss with cookie dough, you can provide play dough or modeling clay for Station 3 just as easily.

Involving taste and smell helps provide sensory input into the task of remembering letters. Using a gingerbread or sugar cookie recipe, you can give each child a piece of dough and ask the child to create the shape of the letter and then decorate it, perhaps with sugar sprinkles, chocolate chips, or raisins. This is something that every child enjoys.

Make sure that children get their own cookies. I cut aluminum foil into squares, print the children's initials in the corners with a permanent felt pen, place the cookies on the foil, and then put them on the cookie sheet. This would work well with parchment baking paper, too.

Typically, a volunteer goes to an oven in the staff room to bake the cookies. The "cooking" is often done around a recess time, and even a helpful principal or two has been known to cheerfully take the cookies out when the buzzer sounds.

Station 4: Designing a focus letter necklace or bracelet

If you are teaching students about patterning in math, this is a good opportunity for students to mix Cheerios and Fruit Loops to make consistent patterns in their necklaces.

If your school has a die cutter for letters, this makes creating letters easier, but if it doesn't, you will need to have the focus letter either cut out or ready to cut out of manila tag or other sturdy paper. Punch a hole at the top of the letter to put the string through so the letter will hang from the centre of this necklace.

Provide stickers, felt markers, small beads, and sparkles to decorate the letter that has already been strung on the string. Provide Fruit Loops and Cheerios, too, to string alongside the letter to make a more detailed necklace. You can fold a piece of masking tape over the string to make a label onto which to print the child's name. Boys, as well as girls, love this activity.

Station 5: Making a focus letter booklet

For this station have a number of simple booklets made out of a standard piece of white paper folded and given a construction paper cover. Beyond that, provide items or pictures of items whose names begin with the focus letter and the names of those items on little cards or labels so that students can see each one and its name. These can be set on a table. Or, set out a number of alphabet books and picture dictionaries for students to look up the focus letter and find the items whose names begin with that letter. For example, for the letter *C* you might have a comb, can, and little car, and pictures of a cat, clock, and candy.

Students are asked to print their names and draw the letter on their booklet covers. They then draw a picture of each item, one to a page. They may print the word that goes with the picture on the page as well. Encourage students to add details to their pictures.

Station 6: Focus letter sort

For this station, provide at least 100 letters. I have used old display letters from bulletin boards, magnetic letters, Scrabble tiles, letter stickers, and even building block letters. I also print about 40 of the focus letters on little cards or 2 cm squares of paper. These letters can be used for many learning activities during the year.

For this activity, each student gets a sheet of paper, searches for five examples of the focus letter, and then arranges them in a special way to make a design or picture on the paper. You could increase the number of letters if the student has more time. If you have many paper letters, you could have the students glue them on the paper, but I usually ask them to make an arrangement so that the letters can be used again. If they have extra time, students could make words of items that begin with the focus letter by looking through picture dictionaries.

REFLECTING ON THE LEARNING

While students are working on these tasks, there will be lots of discussion between the students working at each of the stations. You will be hearing students discussing the items that they are drawing, or telling each other how many *C*'s they have found, which names of the students in the class begin with that letter, or about what art materials they are using in decorating the focus letter necklace. This informal discussion is what helps them become familiar with the letter and gives many opportunities for them to name the letter they are working with.

Encourage students to talk about what they are doing while working. You can ask questions about the letter to help them see that the focus letter is the same letter even though it may look different in various positions. Here are some questions to ask:

- What letter are you working with?
- Do you know some names of people or things that start with this letter?
- What things do you remember about this letter?

If you have a sharing time where a number of students can talk about what they did at their stations, the students will talk about the letter and show their pictures, cookies, arrangements of the letters, or the circled letters on a list of names, and reveal what they learned.

NOTES ON ASSESSMENT

Eventually, you will check with students to see if they can create the letters you ask for with their pencils on paper or if they can identify the letters on a chart, such as the one at the end of the chapter. There are few prerequisite skills to these activities. Prompts for monitoring recognition of the focus letter are given in "Reflecting on the Learning."

Using Alphabet Books, Raps, and Jives

From their earliest years, when they may cuddle in someone's lap looking at a picture book, children are exposed to print. Some of the books that parents read to their children are alphabet books. The reader will point out the names of the letters and read the rhymes or labels, and through engaging in such bright and lively exposure to pictures, symbols, and the spoken language, children learn their ABC's! In all likelihood children will listen to some rendition of the childhood song about all the letters in alphabetic order. Of course, this doesn't happen for all children, but it does happen for many. In the early primary years, teachers continue to sing songs and read alphabet books to students.

Children also learn their letters by the environmental print around them. How many two-year-olds recognize the *M* for a fast food restaurant with golden arches as a symbol? I remember humoring an energetic three-year-old on a long car trip by teaching him to differentiate between all the gas station signs and letting us know when he saw an Esso station or a Petro-Canada station; although shapes, colors, and pictures were a big part of that identification, some letter recognition was involved as well. Good teachers make sure they use many informal, incidental ways to introduce and reinforce letter recognition and teach students the sound–symbol matches they need for reading and writing.

HOW TO TEACH IT

A variety of activities can be done with alphabet books. With some of my colleagues, I have prepared a list of recommended alphabet books and identified several classroom-tested activities (see page 48).

Another common tool to help students remember the alphabet is an alphabet rap or alphabet jive, derived from alphabet stories. My colleague Heather tells how she could hear children repeating it under their breath as they were printing in their Grade 1 classroom. Kristine found that the children loved to say and act out the jive that she used. Lisa found that when students were lined up waiting for dismissal, the jive was a great way to make the time go faster. Repeated with a definite rhythm in loud voice, soft voice, and in-between voice, students can use the words and rhythm of an alphabet jive to help remember the names of alphabet letters and the sounds they make.

There are many alphabet books, poems, raps, and jives that can be found on the Internet, in books, and in any primary classroom. They are great teaching tools.

Activities for alphabet picture books

Announcing a Visitor: Each student in the class is given a Post-it note and an alphabet book. Students choose the letter that they would like to be the class visitor. They mark the appropriate page of the alphabet book with a Post-it note as a bookmark — any duplication of letters does not matter.

The students sit in a semi-circle with the books in front of them and when it is their turn to announce the visitor, they sit in the speaker chair at the front of the group and tell about the letter without giving its name. The commentary might sound like this: "Our visitor is made of three straight lines. He is the letter at the beginning of *king* and *kangaroo* and he loves to kick. Who is he?"

To make sure that there is active participation, ask the students to trace with a finger the letter on the hands of partners or to whisper it to partners; then, the announcer asks a student to name the letter. He or she then shows the page of the alphabet book that features the letter.

Find the Letter: The teacher or class candidate makes the letter on the chalkboard with a wet paintbrush and then tells the class whether the letter is near the front of their book (beginning of the alphabet), the middle, or the end. You may want to point out the letter on the class alphabet chart to show where it appears within the alphabet. When you say, "Go," the students find the letter in their alphabet books before the chalkboard letter dries up. Students put their finger on the page, and when you say ready, they all show the page they have found. You may also ask for the names of things that begin with the given letter and write these words on the board. Doing so lets students see the letter being made.

Three Clues before You Guess: Students get about two minutes to find a picture in their alphabet books, know what letter the word for that object starts with, and think of three things they know about the item. (You may also want to use picture dictionaries for this activity as the objects will be recognizable; with some alphabet books they are not.) Students then bookmark their pages.

When it is their turn — or you can have them do this with a partner — students identify the letter and give three clues, asking the other person or the class to guess what object they are thinking of.

Alphabet Books

Andreae, Giles, and Guy Parker Rees. *K Is for Kissing a Cool Kangaroo*
Brown, Margaret Wise. *Sleepy ABC*
Ehlert, Lois. *Eating the Alphabet, Fruits and Vegetables from A to Z*
Ferguson, Don. *Winnie the Pooh's A to Zzzz*
Hague, Kathleen. *Alphabears: An ABC Book*
Harrison, Susan. *Alpha Zoo Christmas*
Martin, Jr., Bill, and John Archambault. *Chicka, Chicka, Sticka, Sticka*
Napier, Matt, and Melanie Rose. *Z Is for Zamboni: A Hockey Alphabet*
Pallotta, Jerry. *The Extinct Alphabet Book*
Paul, Ann Whitford, and Maggie Smith. *Everything to Spend the Night from A to Z*
Rosenberg, Amye. *A to Z Busy Word Book*
Ruurs, Margriet, and Dianna Bonder. *A Pacific Alphabet*
Ruurs, Margriet, and Andrew Kiss. *A Mountain Alphabet*

The alphabet rap or jive

See pages 49 to 53 for reproducible pages with an alphabet rap or jive. Students may add pictures related to the text about each letter in the space to the right.

Alphabet raps, sometimes called alphabet jives or chants, are a wonderful tool for students to use to remember the letters of the alphabet and the sounds they make. It is a good idea to use the same symbols for the rap as for alphabet stories. This consistency will help students learn the alphabet letters more quickly and have a story base for remembering the sounds that the letters make.

- Make the rap rhythmic with clapping hands and slapping knees, snapping fingers, and so on. Make the sound of the letter at the end of each rhyme.
- Make a Big Book with a letter for each page and the rhyme written out. The book will quickly become print students can read. Or, make a chart with all the letters and the pictures on display so children can use it as a ready reference.
- Do actions with each letter that help the students move to the sound. Most actions are fairly evident, for example, using a slicing motion with your hand for "cut the apple," or a batting motion with your arm for "bat the ball." Students could do the actions during lines 2 and 3.
- When children have become familiar with the rap using the pictures, have them chant without pictures, just pointing to the alphabet letters on the alphabet chart you will probably have posted on your wall.
- Have students do the chant as a "sponge" activity while they are waiting in line, for example. Let them memorize it by doing it often!
- Start at a different place, for example, at *D* or *K*.

Alphabet Rap or Jive

A says a, A says a Cut the apple, Cut the apple, a-a-a	B says b, B says b, Bat the ball, Bat the ball, b-b-b
C says c, C says c, Cookie crumbs, Cookie crumbs, c-c-c	D says d, D says d, Drag the drum, Drag the drum, d-d-d
E says e, E says e Eat with Eddie, Eat with Eddie, e-e-e	F says f, F says f, Fight the fire, Fight the fire, f-f-f

G says g, G says g, Golden guppy, Golden guppy, g-g-g	H says h, H says h, Happy Harry, Happy Harry, h-h-h
I says i, I says i, In goes pin, In goes pin, i-i-i	J says j, J says j, Jumping jack, Jumping jack, j-j-j
K says k, K says k, Kick the can, Kick the can, k-k-k	L says l, L says l, Lovely lady, Lovely lady, l-l-l

Alphabet Rap or Jive 2

M says m, M says m, Mighty mountains, Mighty mountains, m-m-m	N says n, N says n, Noisy nose, Noisy nose, n-n-n
O says o, O says o, Octopus, Octopus, o-o-o	P says p, P says p, Pass the pan, Pass the pan, p-p-p
Q says q, Q says q, Quiet queen, Quiet queen, q-q-q	R says r, R says r, Red rooster, Red rooster, r-r-r

Alphabet Rap or Jive 3

S says s, S says s, Silly snake, Silly snake, s-s-s	T says t, T says t, Tippy table Tippy table, t-t-t
U says u, U says u, Up umbrella, Up umbrella, u-u-u	V says v, V says v, Valentine, Valentine, v-v-v
W says w, W says w, Wacky wings, Wacky wings, w-w-w	X says kiss, X says kiss, X is it, X is it, x-x-x

Alphabet Rap or Jive 4

Y says y,	Z says z,
Y says y,	Z says z,
Yackety-yak,	Zip the zipper,
Yackety-yak,	Zip the zipper,
y-y-y	z-z-z

The Vowels

a	e	i	o	u

The Consonants

b	c	d	f	g
h	j	k	l	m
n	p	q	r	s
t	v	w	x	y
z				

Alphabet Rap or Jive 5

Vowel Stories

a

a is an apple
with a slice
out of it.

e

e is Eddie
who eats and eats
but hates broccoli
and says "egh"
when you feed it
to him.

i

i is a pin
that goes
straight in.

o

o is Ollie
the Octopus
who gets caught
in a net and says,
"ah" in relief
when the fisher
throws him
overboard.

u

u is an upside-down
umbrella.

Assessment Checklist for Recognizing the Alphabet

Name ______________________ Date ______________________

	Name	*Sound*	*Word*		*Name*	*Sound*	*Word*	*Comments*
b				B				
e				E				
f				F				
h				H				
k				K				
l				L				
m				M				
n				N				
a				A				
d				D				
o				O				
v				V				
c				C				
s				S				
z				Z				
w				W				
g				G				
i				I				
j				J				
r				R				
p				P				
y				Y				
x				X				
q				Q				
u				U				
t				T				

Note: The main thing is that the letters are in random order so that students are not relying on their knowledge of alphabet songs or chants.

Checking Alphabet Recognition

Show only one line of print and point to each letter.

Questions to ask:

Do you know the name of this letter?

If the student doesn't, ask the following two questions and place *S* for sound or *W* for word if the student knows the answer to either of the two.

- Do you know what sound this letter makes?
- Do you know a word that has this letter in it?

An answer to any of the three questions shows alphabetic knowledge about that letter.

3

Incorporating Basic Tools into Routines and Play

Two central beliefs about educational environments for young children guide the activities in this chapter. One belief is that early primary classrooms are places where students do much of their learning through play; the other is that young children need predictable, daily routines to shape their day. In this way, students learn in a safe environment where they often know what is going to happen next. During daily routines and centres, teachers can find many opportunities to do some incidental teaching of Basic Tools for writing.

Play is often provided during centre time, a designated time of day where students choose to go to an area where they can play with materials such as blocks, art and craft supplies, and child-sized kitchen utensils; at other centres, materials are provided and children use their imaginations to have fun with their friends. Often the teacher will suggest activities that could be done at a centre and introduce new items for the students' use. The students, however, are usually free to choose what they would like to do at a centre and the teacher's role is to facilitate rather than to teach.

Learning takes place as students imaginatively take on roles and play with their peers, often using the Basic Tools introduced during instructional times to do some writing or to exercise the muscles that will help their fine motor skills. So, little builders make plans with paper and pencils; waitresses record orders from potential clients, stretching out words and hearing and recording sounds; and students develop fine motor skills as they glue together recycled paper rolls, little boxes, and pieces of paper to make toys of their own. Using the suggested activities and materials outlined in this chapter will help to encourage students to practise the Basic Tools.

One routine that specifically helps students learn Basic Tools for writing is the Morning Message.

The Morning Message

In early primary classrooms there are specific routines that start the morning off for children in a predictable way. Along with good morning songs, chants, and the calendar, there is the Morning Message. The Morning Message is a few short lines written on the board by the teacher; it contains some new information

Cloze activities help students to predict a word from the context of a sentence or story. They help students recognize that sometimes just knowing the first letter or other letters of a word can help them choose a word that will make sense in the sentence. Often, they choose a word that looks right as well: one that contains the letters that match the sounds they hear.

about what will happen during the day and usually familiar phrasing that is consistently repeated each day. Through this informal practice, teachers and children discuss how print works, where sentences begin, how spaces are made between words, what phonemes, or letter sounds, they hear at the beginnings and ends of words, and what letters make those phonemes.

As students become increasingly proficient at reading this Morning Message, the teacher turns it into a cloze activity, where little fill-in-the-space blank lines are used to indicate letters that are missing and children supply the missing letters in words they are familiar with. Since many anchor words, such as *it, is, can, like, and, the, will,* and *we,* are commonly used, students are encouraged to learn the spellings of these little words so that they can write them quickly from memory. Morning Message ensures that students are interactively involved in at least one writing activity every day.

As well as doing Morning Message together, students will be seeing their teacher model writing stories and making lists and diagrams, and perhaps even reporting the news of exciting classroom events or field trips, or other shared experiences. During much of this writing the teacher will not have the time to talk about all the concepts of print students need to learn about, although she may ask for some interactive writing and make incidental teaching points about print formation or sound–symbol matches. Morning Message need not be lengthy and should be followed up by many demonstrations of longer, more in-depth writing during the day.

In this chapter, four levels of Morning Message are outlined with some specific teacher talk given to demonstrate how to proceed. These activities are not lessons as such so the assessment ideas and adaptations provided as part of the lessons in other chapters are not here. Morning Message is a daily routine with informal teaching about how talk is written down and what standard forms of written English look like.

The speed at which children will progress through these stages will be different for all classrooms. If children find it very easy and show signs of getting bored, you need to make the task more challenging. There are many variations of what you can do and later in the chapter, a list of prompts and activities to provide variety for students appears.

It is during Morning Message that time is taken to ensure that students witness the process of properly punctuating text. At this time, teachers can talk out loud about the capitals at the beginning of sentences and the periods at the end. The width of a chalk brush or perhaps a modeling clay "meatball" may show the spacing between words, reminding students how letters in words almost touch and that words have spaces between them.

Morning Message can also provide other opportunities. Teachers may stretch out the sounds of the letters in the words they point to and have children do it with them — students are quick to say what word has been stretched out audibly. Teachers may talk out loud about sentences, repeat them, and ask, "Does this make sense?" And when children say it does make sense, they can respond by saying, "Then if it gives a message that makes sense, it must be a sentence!"

Morning Message is great in Kindergarten and beginning Grade 1, but when students learn to read and write more proficiently, this time is best used for other activities. The time dedicated to Morning Message should be about 10 or 15 minutes; at the beginning of Kindergarten, it should take only five minutes or so. Below is a typical Morning Message for an early Kindergarten classroom.

A Stage One Morning Message

Good morning boys and girls.
Today we will go to the gym.

Stage One: Two Lines of Print

Although *Good morning, boys and girls* should have a comma after *morning* to be correct, you might want to leave this comma out until the students have been introduced to commas. Then, you can discuss how this salutation should really have a comma after *Good morning*.

When students first come to school, two lines of print are sufficient for a Morning Message. *Good morning boys and girls* is a very typical way to start. A second line begins with something like *Today we will* and identifies an activity the students will do that day. The two sentences should remain the same for at least two months or perhaps longer.

To begin, it is best to model the writing in front of the children and to talk out loud about your thinking as you write. The dialogue you would be having with the students would sound something like this:

"I am going to write my morning greeting down. It is *Good morning boys and girls.* When we write in English, we always start at the left side and go to the right side. I have to think of what sound I hear at the beginning of *Good* and what letter makes that sound." Sound it out slowly and write it out.

"I make a spaghetti space between the letters. I also need to make a space between my words and so I will make a meatball-sized space. Morning ... mmm. I know that is an *m.* I will write *morning* next."

If you teach students to have their chalkboards ready in front of them while sitting in a semi-circle, you can soon have them printing the letter at the beginning of *morning* or printing the word *we* on their chalkboards while you do Morning Message. Even if you haven't had lessons on how a *w* is printed, they will have seen you model it many times.

Continue in this way until you write the whole sentence with some emphasis on the beginning sounds of words. Make sure that you don't make this an ordeal by spending too much time or making the story too lengthy. Do a bit of instruction every day and let skills build up over time.

After you have done this for a few days, ask students to tell you what sound and what letter makes the sound that *Good* or *morning* or *boys* or *girls* starts with and have them tell you orally or perhaps print it in the air or on their hands with their pointer fingers. It will not be long before students will be able to spell *we* and *will* out loud for you.

Stage Two: Introducing Cloze

After your students have had some time in Kindergarten, you can add another line of print or use different beginning sentence frames — it is important to keep students challenged by providing changes in format and having expectations for all of them to take part. Some children will copy their neighbors' letters and words, and this kind of helpful sharing will make sure that all children are involved and active, even if they haven't mastered the letter sounds or remembered spellings. Weaker students can be "partnered" by stronger students who will help them with letters and words.

Certain indicators signal that students are ready for Stage Two Morning Message. By now you should be talking about the sounds at the ends of words as well as the sounds at the beginnings of words, and students should be able to tell you how to spell simple anchor words such as *the, we,* and *will.* In your conversations you will be talking about beginning a sentence with a capital and perhaps putting a period at the end, and be pointing out the differences and similarities between uppercase and lowercase letters. Some of your students will also be making sound–symbol matches in their independent writing work, although few will be putting more than one or two letters for each word.

By now, you will probably have the Morning Message printed on the board for the first one or two familiar lines and then perhaps write a third line in front of your students. For common phrases, you may leave blanks where letters should be at the beginnings and ends of words, and for some very common two- or three-letter anchor words, leave a blank for the middle sound, as well.

Teacher talk for part of the Morning Message illustrated below might go like this:

Progress will increase with active student participation. Having all students write a letter in the air, whisper missing letters to a partner, or print letters on their hands or arms, on their partners' hands or backs, or on a chalkboard will ensure that everyone is involved. Check pages 12 to 13 for ways to make sure that your students are actively involved.

"Can we make good guesses and read the first line of the Morning Message? When I give the signal, let's read it together. Everyone tell me the letter that goes in the space when I touch the board with my chalk. The next sentence is about a bunny. What is the first word? Make the missing letter in the air. I see an *O.* What do you think this next word will be? Make the word with your pointer finger like a pencil, writing it on your arm. Now, whisper the letters out loud when I give the signal. I hear *w* and *e.* Good. Write the next word on your chalkboard. John has written *w i l l.* That spells *will.* Can you write the next word on your chalkboard? Who knows what it will say? Yes, *see.* Who can spell that on their chalkboard? What two letters make the sound /e/?"

A Stage Two Morning Message

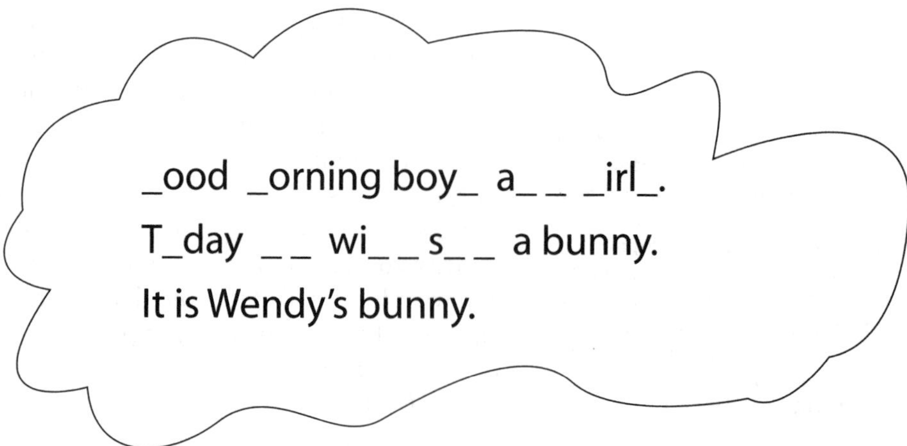

Stage Three: Guiding Practice

At this time you will have children who know a number of simple sight words and who do not need to be reminded daily about spaces between words. They are still not sure of medial vowel sounds, but will know most beginning and ending consonant sounds. They may not be part of formal reading groups, but most children can read simple pattern books and show familiarity with concepts of print, such as how to do a left-to-right sweep and return on the next line to the left-hand side of a page. They track words with their fingers, saying one word out loud to each word they find in text.

Students usually recognize other students' names and by this time of year can write their own names quite quickly and some of the names of their friends. They love having their names up on the board in Morning Message. The more often you can do this the better!

By now you will have introduced some new phrasing to the Morning Message, each phrase being used for a week or two, while you familiarize the students with how to read the phrase, match sounds with letters in predictable words, and learn to spell some anchor words quickly from memory. Instead of "Today we will …," some of these phrases might be "You will like …" "Can you see …?" "Do you want to …?"

Many teachers have students write some of the Morning Message, but I prefer students to write words or part of the Morning Message on their own chalkboards rather than having all the children wait while one student slowly prints. I then borrow a chalkboard and quickly write what the student has written on the board so everyone can check to see if they did it correctly.

A typical conversation concerns something like a bus trip to the farm. On the board you might have a line like this:

__ ____ g__ __n __ b__ __.

You might say:

"You know we are going to the farm and today in our Morning Message we are going to write about that. We are going to write, *We will go on a bus.* Now take up your chalkboard and show me where you will start to write. Good, you found the left-hand side near the top of your board. Remember what we need at the beginning of the sentence and write *We* and now *will.* Let's listen for the sounds in *go.* We have our *g.* Can you print *go* with the next sound you hear in *go* after the *g*? Now, let's think about *on.* What sound do you hear at the beginning of *on*? Can you make that letter in the air with your pointer finger? Good. Now print *on.* Here's a super simple little word — *a.* It's just one letter, and now the last word in our sentence is *bus.* Let's put our chalk down, and stretch out the sounds. *Bbbbb uuuuu sssss.* It has three sounds and the *b* is already here and there is a space for the next two letters that make the rest of the word. Say It Slow and Write It. Now, we are at the end of our sentence. What do we need? That's right — a period.

"When I give the signal, read your sentence out loud and do it in a soft voice. Now, Bobby, let me borrow your chalkboard and I will copy what you have written on the board. Let's read it together. Check your work. Were you able to write the part about going on the bus? Did you leave a meatball space between your words? Check. That is good work!"

You might then ask what students would see on the trip and add a sentence or two about that with only a few teaching points perhaps on beginning sounds or on putting commas between items in a list. Your Morning Message would look something like this, with the last sentence added after you have finished the first three sentences.

A Stage Three Morning Message

Hi class,

________________ is _ _ _ special _elper.

Y_ _ w_ _ _ like t_ _ farm

_ _ _ _ _ _ g_ _n _ b_ _.

We will see cows, sheep and chickens.

Stage Four: Communicating through Cloze

A common practice in many early primary classrooms is to have a special helper for each day. This student is given special privileges for the day, for example, being first in line or able to write on the board. Make sure that everyone in the class has a turn as a special helper.

At this stage students will have begun to do some early reading and will be well on their way to putting down their thoughts on paper in emergent writing. Morning Message is often given to the students as a photocopied cloze exercise for them to fill in, and teacher and students go over it together as part of their morning routine. The purpose of Morning Message tends to become less about looking at the way print works and more about communicating important information about the day to the students. For cloze, the message still needs to follow a somewhat predictable format, while you might add a sentence or two to expand on what you want children to know about the day.

Sometimes, a particular student, or special helper, writes *Hi, class,* and then one or two of the sentence structures you have been using, for example: *Today is Tuesday.* I recommend that this writing be done while the rest of the students are doing something else.

Below is an example of a predictable cloze Morning Message that you could photocopy for each child to fill in as a morning job. When you meet on the carpet, go over the Morning Message, reading it together and filling in the blanks as you go. Students then check to see if they have done it correctly and fill in the spaces they may have left blank.

In the example below, it would be expected that students are familiar with the word *snow* and the questions about things they like and wear. Students would not be given this message without a fair amount of exposure to words such as *boots, snow,* and *wear. Do, did, you,* and *out* would be anchor words learned through Morning Messages in the past.

A Stage Four Morning Message

December _____, __________.

H_ cl_ _ _,

I_ i_ sn_ _ ing _ _ _ side,

D_ y_ _ wear b_ _ ts?

D_ y_ _ li_ _ sn_ _?

Ways to Provide Variety to Morning Message

Your students may show signs of Morning Message "fatigue" or perhaps you want to ensure that they have a more detailed view of the happenings in your neighborhood, country, or beyond. Outlined below are variations and additional activities you can do with Morning Message. These will help provide variety and challenge.

News of the Day: Some teachers don't have a Morning Message; they have News of the Day. The students or sometimes a student chosen earlier to be the "special" student of the day will bring the class news they have been asked to think about or research. It may be news of the world, news of the neighborhood, or personal news. The teacher writes down what the child reports, talks about the writing and makes some teaching points about spacing, beginning sounds, and so on. After the news of two or three sentences is written, the children and teacher read it together. You may then ask students to read it individually, identify certain words, or identify letters after you have rubbed the first letters of a few words off the board. The text is personal and relevant and makes for a great teaching tool.

Cut-up Chart Story: If Morning Message or News of the Day is written on chart paper, there are some advantages. One activity that can be done after it has been filled in (if there are fill-in-the-blank spaces) is to cut it up and create a puzzle. Students can put the message back together either in a pocket chart or on the floor. Initially, you just cut the sentences apart and students make sure that the Morning Message begins with the salutation to the class and has the correct sequence of sentences.

Later, you can cut up the message in phrases or in separate words that need to be put together. Doing this has many advantages. Students need to make sure that the sentence starts with a word that has a capital and ends with punctuation, such as a period. Students have to remember what word comes next in the sentence they are re-creating. If the sentences are cut up in phrases, students can practise reading their re-created story in fluent phrases. For example in the marked-up sentence below, the students would be encouraged to read each section smoothly, saying the words in each phrase all together quickly with miniscule pauses between the phrases to ensure that they learn to read with fluency instead of word by word. When asking students to read with fluency, tell them to "make it sound like talking."

Lots of people *cut* / lined up *cut* / to see the Queen.

This activity can be done at a learning centre later on in the day rather than during Morning Message.

Take Home Message: What better way to help parents know about what is happening in school than to give those parents a chance to read the Morning Message with their child? The special helper may take the Morning Message or News of the Day home to keep and then have a lot of fun reading it to parents and siblings, copying it, cutting it up to make a puzzle, and more.

Morning Message Books: Some teachers always photocopy the Morning Message and as students become more proficient, they complete the cloze sentences by filling in missing letters and words, and even independently writing a sentence to finish the story. Every week these little stapled-together books go home, providing parents with news about the week and opportunities to discuss what students are learning about writing.

I Spy: When the Morning Message is written, children can take turns thinking about a specific word and giving clues, or the teacher can give clues and ask students to make a guess about a specific word. For example: "I spy with my little eye a word that begins with *m* and tells about a time of day."

You can ask students to circle the word on the chart paper or chalkboard. Again, even if one child comes up to circle it, it is a good idea to have students whisper the word to partners first to ensure that there is active participation. If students are more advanced, you can ask them to write the word on their chalkboards, and give them just a minute to do so. This helps to keep everyone involved.

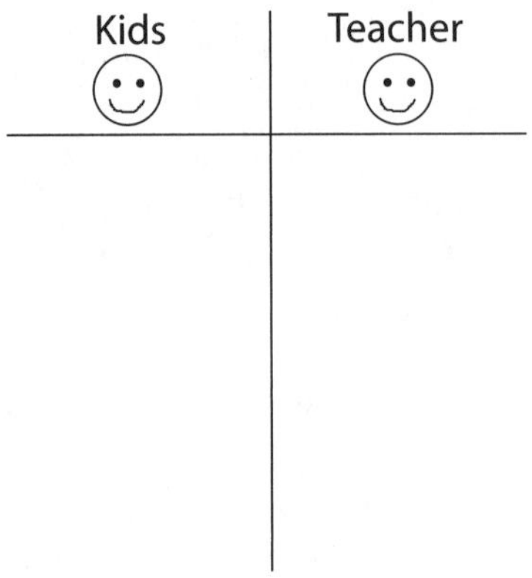

Kids ☺	Teacher ☺

Kids versus the Teacher Game: This game is always popular in the classroom and can be used in a variety of settings, Morning Message being one. Start by drawing a T-chart on the board, and label one side Kids and the other side Teacher. The rules of the game are simple. Call on a student, circle a word, wait for five seconds, and then rub the word off. Count to five slowly in a whisper, and if the student has not said the word, say it and get a point. If the student says it correctly in the time allotted, the Kids get the point. If anyone else shouts out or whispers the word to the person who is It, you get a point.

This is one time when the children cannot help each other, but be careful to match the word to the ability of the particular child. Of course, the Teacher always loses. I like to make this more dramatic by putting happy faces at the top of the tally columns and say this is because the Kids think they will win the game, and the Teacher thinks she will win the game; at the end, I turn the Teacher's happy face into a sad one with huge tears coming down, and tell them I'm so sad because I lost. I then revert to being happy because I know everyone is learning so much! No matter how many times I tell them this silly story, they laugh. Young children like predictable events!

Morning Message can be a valuable learning time for all students. Because it is short, interactive, and predictable, it can be an activity that takes teachers little time to prepare and yet allows students to learn a lot.

Students also learn a great deal during another time of the day where the emphasis is not on instructing students on Basic Tools, but rather on providing play materials for students to have fun. Centres, where students play together, provide opportunities for students to practise Basic Tools and for teachers to encourage and comment on their use.

Writing in Centres

When we provide space, opportunity, and supplies for students to write as they play — as well as encouragement and modeling — we are providing tools for young children to learn in the best way possible: through their imaginations as they interact with their peers.

A series of suggestions follow. They show how providing ideas, materials, and role-playing opportunities in the centres found in Kindergarten and Grade 1 classrooms can help students do the practice and exploration that all young writers need. Some centres are traditional ones found in most early primary classrooms: the home centre, the blocks centre, and the easels centre. With a little teacher guidance and the provision of the right materials, these centres are great places for students to practise the Basic Tools they have been learning about.

Other centres are literacy centres, where the focus is on letters, reading, writing, and spelling tasks that students do independently as a free choice. The list is not exhaustive, but you may find confirmation of some of the ideas you are now using, as well as one or two new ideas that students will find entertaining and useful.

Students, of course, want to spend their time playing, creating, and making things more than they want to write about their experiences. So, it is best to slot 5 to 10 minutes just before clean-up time for them to do their writing, which becomes their ticket for sharing what they have made. Students will choose some pencil-and-paper tasks as part of their play if they have a chance to report on what they did in centres with pictures, models, stories, and so on as part of their sharing time. Sharing the experiences they have in a classroom is often more valuable to students than taking part in other kinds of Show and Tell activities where they bring things from home.

Translation: I am going to my grandma's right after school.

The Blocks Centre

Students need modeling and rules before they begin to work in centres, and good teachers often suggest and demonstrate things that students might build. Although students have lively imaginations and will work happily on their own, learning is enhanced when a teacher acts as a facilitator, commenting and providing needed language to the work students are doing, asking questions so students see relationships between objects and events, and coming up with ideas for students to extend their knowledge and experience. Below are some suggestions that will help students spend some of their time at the blocks centre doing pencil-and-paper tasks that help with writing.

Making blueprints

If you have blueprints of a house or building, these are wonderful to share with students, and having some large pieces of paper, drafting rulers, and T-squares will encourage students to draw blueprints of their buildings before they start. Of course, blueprints may also require some signs, numbers, and measurements. Although I would want the students to "play" at making blueprints without my necessarily having a lot of expectations, having an Architect at Work badge and the materials for drafting will appeal to many of the children.

Count it up sheet

This simple little sheet has a picture of the blocks on one side and a place for numbers beside each picture of each block. The students simply count up the number of blocks they used in their structure and record it on the sheet. This then becomes the "ticket" for them to share their experience with the class.

Our team: __________ __________ __________ __________

We made a ______________________.

This is what we used:

__________ __________ __________

Somewhat similarly, students could make small creatures or items with recycled paper, paper-towel tubes, lids, spools, easily bent wire, Popsicle sticks, and more at a make-it centre; then, on a simple form you provide, they could print the words or draw the objects they used. Providing a chart with pictures and words of items such as scissors and glue would help.

Making signs

Having cardboard, manila tag, and felt markers available to make signs is a great idea. Having strips of black paper for highways is also a good idea, and it is wonderful to see students using yellow chalk to make dotted lines, double lines, and left-turn lanes. As children draw these lines, they are practising the fine motor skills they need for writing and using their observation skills, as well. Modeling clay, transparent tape, and chopsticks can be used to make signposts.

The Home Centre

The home centre usually has a play refrigerator, a stove, dolls, dishes, a table and chairs, and sometimes dress-up clothes so that children can play parents. Often, students are relegated to be the dog. Every Kindergarten teacher, I'm sure, has had to warn students that dogs shouldn't bark loudly in the house! Sometimes, the space in the home centre becomes a restaurant or a shopping centre and these provide opportunities for writing.

The shopping list

A magnetized shopping list is great if you have a place to put it and a pencil tied to it. Another good idea is a whiteboard on the side of the refrigerator, or a little box with a pencil or two and a shopping list format on pieces of paper. If you have a classroom "store," be sure to prompt students to make lists before they go there. Even if students do pretend writing or put in first letters of items they want, this represents good thinking. Drawing pictures is a great way to make an itemized list as well. Make sure that students who draft shopping lists can talk about about their items during a sharing time.

A to-do list

I have often told students that my children and I spent every Saturday morning doing housework and then had a "treat" in the afternoon to celebrate what we had accomplished. I explained how we had a to-do list and the one request my son would always make was not to add jobs once the list was made.

In like fashion, you could suggest students think of jobs that could be done in the home centre: dust the furniture, cook the dinner, feed the cat, take out the garbage. Having a little box of paper available, encouraging students to make to-do lists, and allowing them to tell the story of how their "child" did his or her tasks will help students decide this is worth doing. Many of them do "pretend" writing or make pictures, but some will use their letter sounds to write.

A tea party

Sometimes, I bring in a special tablecloth, a china teapot, and china teacups and saucers. Two students make place cards with students' names and a little menu sheet for the table, and then they invite two or four persons to tea. I usually bring in tea biscuits, and they add play dough or "pretend" items to the menu as well. Serving cold iced tea in china cups has never once resulted in breakage. Students practise printing each other's names and have a great time!

The Easels Centre

Often, when people think of Kindergarten, they picture a student at the easel with a fat paintbrush and a look of concentration, painting in an uninhibited fashion. When a few items other than paint and paper are added to the easels, teachers can ensure that students also do some writing.

The sentence strips

I used to ask students to tell me the stories that accompany their paintings and I wrote the stories on sentence strips which were then stapled on to the paintings; now, however, I ask them to write independently on the sentence strips provided. Sentence strips can be made out of drawing paper and cut to the same width as students' paper for painting. I place them in a box or windowsill near the easels centre, along with a box of crayons or felt markers.

The labels

Providing a nearby list of labels with little pictures helps students to label some items in their pictures. They need to read the labels with the help of the pictures and then use pencil to copy the word off the label. Typical labels are sun, clouds, flowers, people, me, house, friend, trees. Having students print the words helps them with fine motor skills and learning to read and write those words. After a while, you may invite them to label objects in "kidwriting."

The Post Office Centre

The children would make stamps on a sheet of paper at another time and then cut the small squares out and put them in a box, ready for pasting.

My colleague Heather found that one of her most successful centres was the post office. There was a letter carrier who delivered letters to students' individual cubbies every day and lots of writing paper and stamps. To access the stamps you had to key in a special Personal Identification Number (PIN) on the little computer under the stamp box. Having a daily PIN number and small calculators around were handy for number recognition and something students enjoyed working with.

The letters were designed for young writers with a *Dear* _____, a body with lines, and *With Love* __________ at the bottom. The post master had a "stamp" to cancel the stamp on the letter and then put it in the mailbox. The post office also accepted letters to principals, janitors, and other teachers. Students wrote letters of appreciation or apology where needed. Heather, of course, wrote letters to students as well and carefully monitored that no child felt left out due to receiving too few letters.

Literacy Centres

The centres outlined below are more closely aligned with the instructional tasks associated with becoming literate. Types of literacy centres include the writing centre, the alphabet centre, and the students–teacher centre.

The writing centre

A table with many kinds of paper and little booklets, some cards whose flowers and pictures you can cut out and paste on notes, folded cardstock or writing paper, an array of markers, crayons, felt pens and even ballpoint pens and pencils, a few stickers, some envelopes ... this is a place where you can recycle envelopes from junk mail, old cards, and the pretty but never-used writing paper from an aunt, while bringing someone pleasure and a chance to learn.

Children need to see models of what their writing should look like and how to fill four pages in a little booklet. Unless you set expectations for the use of the materials you will find that students create 10 letters at one go with just the word *Hi* written inside, and half of your pretty paper will be used in a single day. For booklets, I often print the words *First, Then, Next,* and *Finally* so that they know they have to create a single event story.

For the seasons, consider getting volunteer parents to help make booklets in the shapes of pumpkins, ghosts, Santa Claus, or snowmen. The children love them, and of course they are easy to share with other students.

The alphabet centre

When you and the students have studied a printed-out poem or short story, a great idea is to cut it up and put all the manila tag strips into a zip-lock bag; children can then re-construct it later on the floor or a table. This is an easy-to-create centre where students have to remember, think, sequence, and read. It is more a reading centre than a writing centre, but in early years these activities reinforce each other well.

This simple centre contains a box of letters, perhaps construction paper ones left over from bulletin-board displays; it may also have magnetic letters, letters on stickers, old Scrabble tiles, and other letter game letters. Once, I had an overhead projector where students could make words with the magnetic letters and project them on the wall.

Here, students can also glue paper letters onto paper to make people's names and words. The only rule is that these are proper words they can read. Having picture dictionaries nearby and charts of student names helps ensure that students have lots of references. Although some students choose this centre as a free choice, I have often treated it as a "have to do" centre with some definite expectations.

The students–teacher centre

This centre is simply made with three student cards stringed so students can wear them like a necklace and one teacher card made in the same way. There will be a small chalkboard or a whiteboard each, some scrap paper and pencils, and perhaps some other items, such as a spelling list and a list of adding and subtracting facts.

The student first serving as teacher chooses to teach one fact to the students, perhaps a word spelling or a numerical fact. Such teachers can use all the examples they like and talk just like an adult teacher, while the students listens. Then the three students are given the word to spell or the fact to write on their chalkboards and the teacher marks it. Usually, the teacher has three facts to teach; then, another student becomes the teacher and on they go.

In the last five minutes, centre members write the words or facts learned on a piece of paper to take to sharing.

Sharing at the end of centre time

This time has to be short and it's difficult to be fair to all the students because it takes too long for everyone to share. Some things, like paintings, may not be dry at the end of the session, so a box where students can put their written stories and pictures when dry and tallies of what they made is a good idea. These items can be shared before students go home.

At the end of centre time, let one or two groups share how they used their time. They can come up as a group with each student telling what she or he did, perhaps having the class do a quick tour to see what was built at the blocks centre, if appropriate. Because a piece of paper with something written on it is a "ticket" to sharing, sharing provides incentive for writing at a centre.

It is often so much easier to ask students to clean up and put away everything they have done, but letting students share their pride in their accomplishments is important, too.

Although time at centres is not time where direct instruction on Basic Tools is provided, students can practise what they have learned in a way that is personal and relevant to them. Learning is enhanced when the idea for writing comes from the students' own needs or imaginations. Making sure students have opportunities and materials handy to write while playing makes good sense.

4

Phonemic Awareness and Sound–Symbol Matches

As an adult user of English, you likely find spelling phonetically easy. Someone tells you to spell *cat* and you sound it out. Your thoughts would go something like this: "Well, I hear a /cccc/ sound. That's made by the letter *c*. Then an /aaaa/ sound — that's made by the letter *a* — and at the end a /ttt/ sound — that's a letter *t*." And so there you have it. You can make the sounds, know the letters that make each sound, and write them down in the sequence you hear. That's easy for you, but difficult for a beginning writer. The fact that a /kk/ sound can be made by a *c* or a *k* is only a small part of the problem.

The small units of speech that correspond to letters of an alphabetic writing system are phonemes. Students have difficulty separating a word into phonemes, so they often don't hear *c*, *a*, and *t* as separate sounds. Some of them don't know about position words and are then confused when you refer to beginning sounds, sounds in the middle, and sounds at the end. This means that position words need to be learned, and it doesn't help that the *c* in *cat* could be described in any of the following ways: the first, the one at the beginning, at the start, or number one. There isn't always consistency in how we talk about the position of sounds in words. Students have to learn all the position words and translate what that means when it comes to words on paper. There are also two-letter phonemes, such as /sh/ and /th/ and /er/, silent letters, such as *gh* in *light*, as well as all the variations that vowel sounds make to consider. Not only do students need to sound out words; they also need to rely on visual memory in order to spell. It's not simple.

A little saying that helps students remember the difference between phonemes (letter sounds) and letters goes like this: "We hear phonemes with our ears and see letters with our eyes." The words *phonemes* and *letter sounds* are used interchangeably throughout this book.

Still, despite the drawbacks, in order to write a word they don't know by memory, the best tool children can use is to say the word slowly, separate the sounds, and put down the letters that match the sounds in the order that the phonemes are made. If the spellings that come from this method aren't conventional, they are often at least readable.

In this chapter, there are lessons to assist students in being able to hear the individual phonemes in words, learn about the positions of phonemes in words, separate the phonemes in short words, and match the phonemes they hear with letters they know. It is expected that students will have had much practice with phonemes and knowing what letters make those sounds. They need phonemic awareness, or the ability to manipulate the phonemes that make up words, in order to become good spellers and readers.

Phonemic awareness includes the ability to recognize and create rhyming words. Although this chapter has no lessons specifically on rhyming, it is helpful for students to have many experiences in finding words that rhyme, creating rhyming words in couplets, supplying rhyming words in interactive poems, and listening to and enjoying rhyming poems, games, and songs.

Phoneme, Word, or Sentence?

Before we write we often think of the words we want to write. Our inner thoughts are like talk. Writing is talk written down. We talk in sentences made up of individual words, and words are made up of the smallest of speech sounds: phonemes. Helping students understand these concepts is a beginning step in their understanding the importance of listening to the speech sounds of words they are attempting to write for their compositions.

EXPLORING THE PURPOSE

When students who are unfamiliar with what the word *cat* looks like go to spell it, they have to rely on hearing and recording the sounds they hear in the word. They need to know that the sound /k/ is represented by either a *c* or a *k* and they need to write it down and get ready for the next sound they hear. They need to know that in speech there are letter sounds, words, and sentences. This lesson helps them differentiate between these kinds of speech sounds.

GETTING READY

Choose objects that make sounds students hear in the classroom every day, for example, a stapler stapling a paper, a piece of chalk marking a chalkboard, a door slamming, a book closing, a paper being crumpled, a timer buzzing. Be ready to play a guessing game. Have categories listed on the board or chart paper with space underneath for words to be printed. These categories would be Not a Speech Sound, Words, Phonemes, and Sentences (if you plan to introduce sentences during this lesson).

HOW TO TEACH IT

Begin by introducing the students to non-speech sounds: paper crinkling, lights switching on and off, hands clapping, a stapler stapling, and chalk squeaking on a chalkboard. Having all the children sitting with their eyes covered and identifying these sounds is great fun. Tell them that these are all sounds you have made with things, or, if you think they can answer it, ask, "How are all these sounds alike?" (Most Kindergarteners would find this a difficult question.)

Then, make some sounds with your mouth: *ha, ha, sh! Sh! Ow! Ow! Cluck, cluck,* and so on, and ask how these sounds are alike. The students should tell you that you've made them with your mouth. You may also ask if these sounds have a message, for example, what it means when you say *sh!* or *ow!* Again, they should be able to tell they have meaning.

The next question to ask is "Are these sounds words?" There might be some confusion, which is all right. It gets students thinking about what a word is. This category could be called speech sounds that have meaning, but are not words.

Give another set of sounds that are definitely words, for example, *stop, bed, bug, eraser, pen, jump,* and *run,* and ask students what they have in common.

They should be able to tell you that they are words. Again, ask if they have meaning. Do the students know what you are talking about?

Then, produce other sounds, such as /b/, /t/, /w/, /f/, /r/, and /c/, and ask students if they know what they have in common. Are they words? Do students understand what to do when they hear them? Do they have meaning? They usually tell me that they are letters and don't have meaning. I tell them that when we talk about the sounds that letters make when all on their own, they are called phonemes.

Depending on your group you might want to introduce sentences another day, but if your students are in Grade 1 or later, you can also introduce sentences in this lesson. You could say:

"Listen to these sounds. How are they alike? Go to the store. Sit up and listen. The dog went down the street. Mrs. White has a brown cat."

Elicit from the students that these are words put together in sentences and that sentences usually make sense and give a message.

There is a danger of students confusing the written aspect of letters and words with speech sounds.

To help students understand what a sentence is, you could introduce the Messenger game. Taking the role of messenger, at the door, knock loudly, announce a sentence or sentence fragment with a flourish, and ask students to put their thumbs up if they thought it was a sentence or thumbs down if they thought it wasn't. Did it provide a message that made sense? You could give them fragments or sentences such as the following: in the street; John Alexander, who is Mary's younger brother; a car is blocking the driveway; the green ribbon in her hair; a woman wants to have dinner ready when she gets home.

Review the lesson so far by asking students to think back and give four examples for each category. Print their responses under each category. Do not emphasize the letter–sound relationship because the purpose of this lesson is hearing sounds, not recording them. Recording, however, is a useful and important tool because the visual aspect of phonemes, words, and sentences helps students understand the "size" of the speech sound. Below is what this chart might look like:

Not a Speech Sound	Word	Phonemes	Sentences
Paper crinkling	go	t	I can ride fast.
Stapler stapling	ball	f	Joe is at the store.
Door slamming	Mary	sh	The dog is a German Shepherd.
Feet stepping	wish	k	Go down to the basement.
Timer buzzing	red	l	Here is the hammer.

The game

When students understand the above information, they are ready to play Phoneme, Word, or Sentence. They answer by raising the appropriate number of fingers. For a phoneme, which is the smallest, they raise one finger; for a word, they raise two fingers; and for a sentence, they raise all five fingers. This is a quick way for them to show their knowledge and understanding. Once students have had lots of opportunity to practise with you, ask them to play the game in partners.

When students play this game in pairs, there will be students unable to come up with a phoneme, word, or sentence on their own. These students will need to be recognized and set up for further practice and coaching. In the meantime, I often give such students a suggestion of a

Here is a short list that you can use with the students as you play this game: Sit, /t/, /s/, green, stop, The train is coming, /g/, pretty, /m/, happy, I am going to school today.

REFLECTING ON THE LEARNING

Tell the students that they have learned a lot about different kinds of speech sounds and encourage them to tell you what kinds of speech sounds these are. ne prompts to use are these:

Give me an example of a phoneme.
Is /t/ a phoneme or a word? (If the student can distinguish it successfully, say he or she seems to understand what a phoneme is.)
Give me an example of a word.
Make a sound that is not a speech sound.
Give me an example of a sentence.
What is usually longer — a phoneme or a word?
What is usually longer — a sentence or a word?

rever possible tell students what they seem to understand or what they v, so they have a clear idea of what kind of learning they have done.

S ON ASSESSMENT

e the Lesson: If students are unfamiliar with the idea of categorizing, some eaching may be required. For example, consider the phrase "in common" as Vhat do these sounds have in common or what is the same about these ls?" A typical Kindergarten game consists of showing a number of items elong to a particular category, for example fruits, and then showing an item loesn't belong, such as a pencil with the fruits, and asking, "Which one 't belong?" Teachers often use this game as a way to help students learn to rize and to learn the language of categorization that leads to phrases such common," or "belong together," or "separate from the others." It is ed that students will know these concepts for the above lesson, but be sure blish whether or not they are familiar with these terms first.
lents will also have to know one finger, two fingers, and all five fingers, and to understand the match between a phoneme and one finger, a word and gers, and a sentence for five fingers. Most students will not find this diffi- it be aware that there may be students who cannot do this.

the Lesson: Assessment is done as students play the Phoneme, Word, or e game, but make sure that students can match numbers of fingers to the itegories. Sometimes, the directions are confusing to the students, but sked the direct question "Is this a phoneme, word, or sentence?" they at they do understand the concepts. Taking some time to ask individual the direct questions will help you determine who understands the dif- between the three concepts.

e Lesson: The students will need many opportunities to practise with es, words, or sentences and then their responses can be noted on either ment checklist based on the generic one in the Appendixes or the indi- iecklist provided at the end of this chapter.
mmend assessing student ability to hear and record sounds in words use of a Reading Recovery form devised by Marie Clay. I usually use hat appears in *An Observation Survey of Early Literacy Achievement*

(published by Heinemann in 1993). You dictate a sentence and ask the student to put down any sounds heard. The score is standardized and gives an indication of how a particular student fares. Observing the changes in scores over time and noting which sounds the student can hear and record is an effective assessment tool.

MAKING IT SIMPLER

Choose Only Two Categories: With students younger than Grade 1, you might decide to go more slowly and start with only two categories, for example, non-speech sounds and speech sounds. Students can still play the game with thumbs up or down. Add a category each day — phonemes, words, and sentences — gradually getting them comfortable with categorizing the speech sounds with a show of fingers.

Play Teacher and Students: If students are uncomfortable working in partners, or if you have some non-cooperative or non-verbal students in your class, change the use of partners in this lesson to a teacher-and-students focus. In this game, there are four students: one is the teacher and faces the other three; the other three put up their fingers in response to their teacher's speech sound: phoneme, word, or sentence. At a signal, another student takes a turn being a teacher, but a student may "pass" if unsure. Pairing unsure students with stronger students can help ensure that everyone is comfortable. As "twins," they can work on solutions — how many fingers to put up — together. This activity works best if they have played this game in other situations.

INCREASING THE CHALLENGE

A quick game suggested by a colleague, Carol Jepson, is to ask students for a phoneme, word, or sentence as their "ticket" out the door for recess or at the end of the school day.

- A more difficult game is to ask students to give you a number of items in sequence. For example, you might say, "When I give the signal I want you to give me two phonemes, three words, and one sentence." This makes it an exercise in remembering things in sequence which is also helpful for the task of hearing and recording sounds in words.
- Students may also do the game in partners. A student holds up one finger to signal the need to provide a phoneme, two fingers to provide a word, or three fingers to produce a sentence.

Ghost Talk—Learning to Separate the Phonemes in Simple Words

Young children have difficulty with the concept of a word containing a number of different letter sounds, and listening to identify each one is not easy. As teachers demonstrate in Morning Message and in alphabet work, the first sounds children listen for are at word beginnings; we then generally go to the sounds at the ends of words and ask students to identify them. However, along with beginning and ending sounds, students need to understand the concept of words being made up of a number of letter sounds. One way to identify each individual sound in a word is by introducing Ghost Talk, in which a word is slowly stretched out the way a ghost might.

EXPLORING THE PURPOSE

When children begin to write their stories, they often put down just the first sound or sometimes the first and last sounds they hear in a word. A sentence, such as "I went out to play," might be represented by these letters:

I wt ot t pa.

This is good emergent writing and shows that the student is conscientiously thinking and sounding out each word he or she is writing. But students need to hear all the sounds in a word and have practice breaking a word into all its individual phonemes. By doing this they also learn to put individual phonemes back into a word when they use sounding out as a strategy in reading.

GETTING READY

You can make a stick puppet named Wordy by attaching him to a ruler or other firm handle (see outline, page 90), and children can make similar stick puppets. Wordy is the only object needed for this lesson. You may want to have a list of simple two phoneme and three phoneme words at hand.

HOW TO TEACH IT

Introduce the lesson by telling the students you have a little puppet that is going to help them understand a language made up of English words that you say slowly, dragging out each sound. Tell them it is called Ghost Talk. You might say, "Let's see if you can understand Ghost Talk, because Wordy has something to say to you." Then, stretch out the word *Hello* as *hhhhhheeeeellllloooo,* in a whispery ghost-like voice and ask them if they know what Wordy said. They almost all can tell it is Hello.

Next, tell them that Wordy knows some of their names and stretch out the names of about six students very slowly. I find the students are eager to tell me whose name Wordy is stretching out.

Then, ask them if they can talk to Wordy in Ghost Talk, prompting them first to say, "Hello." They need to be reminded that it's just a sound at a time because most of them will not isolate each sound, but instead say "Hell looo," breaking the word into syllables. At this juncture, with longer words and names, it's more important to let them experiment than to correct them.

Tell students that Wordy is going to say some little words that have only two sounds. He will say them in Ghost Talk and you will check to see if they can tell you the English word. Ask them to think of the first sound they hear in the word and refer them to Morning Message where the focus is often just the first sound. Getting them to isolate the first sound in a word is very helpful.

You can make a little visual on the board like this:

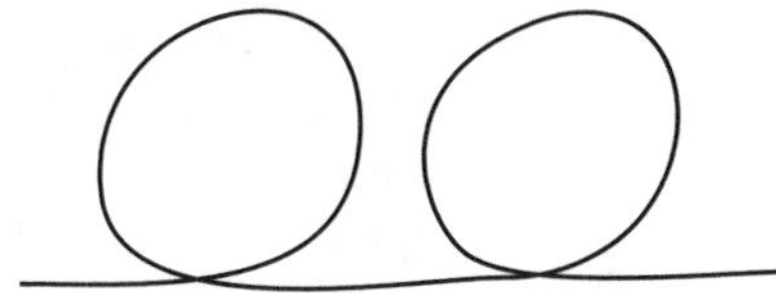

Then say the first sound in the first loop, using your finger or chalk to show how it progresses, and the second sound in the second loop.

Slowly stretch out two phoneme words such as *hi, to, see, it, me, why,* and follow the loops on the board. For each of the stretched-out words you say in Ghost Talk, ask for unison responses in English.

For unison responses I have a signal. When I want students to listen as I stretch out the word, I hold my fist closed in front of them. As soon as I open my fist, they can say the word in English. I tell them that a fist closed is volume off; a fist open is volume on. When I'm training them, I make sure there is a good pause, a count of 1001, 1002, 1003, before turning the volume on (fist open). That way there is a little drama and anticipation!

Next, go on to three phoneme words, such as *cat, dog, sun, hat, tap*, tracing loops on a three-loop diagram, one loop per sound. The three-loop diagram would look like this.

The process is then reversed. Tell students that you are going to say the English word and they need to say the word in Ghost Talk. Give them words with two and three phonemes. I often need to stress that I want to hear the beginning sound first and then the second sound, or for the three phoneme words, the three sounds.

This lesson is all about phonemes, so do not confuse children by writing letters or words on the board. You want them listening, blending phonemes together, and taking English words apart to make the two or three phonemes that make those words.

Next, students could make their own little stick puppets so they can play in partners, with one person saying words in Ghost Talk and the other person saying them back in English, and then perhaps switching.

REFLECTING ON THE LEARNING

At the end of this lesson tell students again why it's fun and helpful to learn Ghost Talk: "We are learning to do this so we can think about and listen for all the letter sounds in words. When we write words we have to be able to say the word slowly so we hear all the sounds in the word including the sound at the beginning, like the *c* in *cat*, and the sound in the middle, like the *a* in *cat*, and the sound at the end, like the *t* in *cat*. When we use Ghost Talk like Wordy, it's easier to hear all the sounds."

After a couple of demonstrations, ask the students to give their partners simple orders, such as sit, stand, or clap, in Ghost Talk. The listening students do the order and if they do it correctly, their partners can raise their hands. Partners can then change roles. Although many will not be able to isolate each phoneme and there will be a need to assess students individually after this display, you may ask: "Who can talk in Ghost Talk?" "Who can understand Ghost Talk?" Compliment students on their learning for the day.

NOTES ON ASSESSMENT

Before the Lesson: A list of words for children to repeat after you will help you determine which speech sounds they may be unable to make. (See the end-of-chapter list.) They will still have fun making Ghost Talk, but will have some difficulty with a few of the individual sounds. Some students may need to learn how to place their lips, tongue, and teeth, as well as understand the difference between voiced and unvoiced sounds (described below), to help them learn how to make some phonemes. Your speech-language pathologist will be able to recommend other exercises that can help students overcome these difficulties.

Students need to know the concept of beginning sound, middle sound, and ending sound to be able to do this lesson effectively. Again, these concepts are taught in Morning Message and with alphabet games. Using the list of words at the end of this chapter and asking students to give you the sound they hear at the beginning of the word will help you determine whether the students will be able to benefit from the Ghost Talk lesson.

During the Lesson: While students are working in pairs, it is helpful to observe them with your checklist of students' names, to listen as they use Ghost Talk to isolate phonemes in words, and to recall their responses when you gave them three letter–phoneme words for Ghost Talk. Note who is having difficulty and plan for more practice. You will need to do this lesson often and to observe those students who can do it effortlessly and those who need a lot of practice.

After the Lesson: During a beginning lesson, it is best to have students observe you modeling and then give many opportunities for practice without doing much assessment. Many of the students will enjoy trying it, but will have difficulty at mastery. Assessment of these skills will come in later lessons.

MAKING IT SIMPLER

Compound Word Game: A good way to help students understand first and last sounds, which is important in this lesson, is to play a game with compound words. You ask the child to repeat the word *blueberry* as an example, and then say "Now say *blueberry* without the *blue*, or say *blueberry* without the *berry*." Ask if *blue* is first or last in *blueberry*. Do this with a number of compound words. This activity helps students understand the concept of separate parts of a word but in a more concrete way than dealing with letter sounds.

Ghost Twins: Some students will be reticent to stretch out words slowly, thinking it a bit silly, or may be reluctant to offer any ideas orally. Tell these students they are "ghost twins" and choose stronger, more forthcoming students to stand with them so that they can do Ghost Talk together. If students are working in partners, the stronger partner can be the "twin," both asking the question and helping to come up with the answer.

Long Beginning Sounds: Many students stretch out the vowel sound and only incidentally connect beginning and ending sounds on the word. Spending time on just two phoneme words helps students get in the habit of separating the first sound from the vowel sound so they hear that *hi* for example is /hhhhh/ first and then /iiii/. Telling them you want to just hear the beginning sound for a long time before you hear the ending sound in a two phoneme word will help. Having students make their own little "loop" cards will also help them know that each phoneme is a loop; they have to trace the loops as they make the words.

Rubber Band Stretch: Sometimes, stretching out a rubber band as you stretch out the words gives the students a visual understanding of what you are attempting to do with the words. Show them how the word is usually a short series of sounds but that you are stretching it to make a long slow series of sounds. You can demonstrate this by using the word *fast*. With the rubber band slack, say "Fast" quickly, then stretch it a little bit and say "Fffaaassstt," and then stretch it as far as you dare and say, "Ffffffaaaaassssssttttttt."

Producing Letter Sounds: Students need to be able to make the phonemes that match letters in order to do this lesson and of course, as seen in preceding chapters, there are many opportunities for students to make these letter sounds as they study printing and learning the letters of the alphabet. It is common for many five-year-olds and some six-year-olds to have difficulty with a number of speech sounds, such as the sounds made by the letters *r, s, l,* and *f*. Many teachers teach each of the letter sounds using a mirror so children can see the placement of tongue, breath, and lips and know how to make an /l/ sound, or that /s/ and /z/, or /b/ and /p/ are made the same way with their teeth and lips in the same position. One is voiced (with the larynx) and the other is unvoiced (no larynx).

For small children, I often say, "Motor on" for a voiced sound and "Motor off" for the unvoiced sound. When students put fingers to their throats, they can tell that the motor is on by feeling the vibration there.

INCREASING THE CHALLENGE

- Some students will need longer words and using the students' names is excellent. They can work in partners using Ghost Talk to stretch out each other's names.
- Using pictures instead of words can increase the level of complexity. Have simple pictures of such things as a fish, a crab, a dog, or a cat. Ask students to say the word in Ghost Talk and then English. See if they can isolate all the sounds.

The Bumping Game — Blending Two Phonemes Together

When children know about phonemes as parts of words and when they have had some practice with Ghost Talk, stretching out the phonemes of a word, they are ready to begin matching the phonemes they hear with their ears and make with their mouths to the letters that represent those phonemes. They need to learn to write them down in the order they hear them in order to make words for writing.

Students love stories, and so I invented a story that helps students understand the concept of two phonemes blending into a simple word.

EXPLORING THE PURPOSE

When students sit down to write a story, there are so many little words they can spell if they are in the habit of stretching out the sounds and putting down the letters of the phonemes they hear. This useful tool enables students to become independent early in the writing process, so taking the time to teach this thoroughly is beneficial. Many students know most of their alphabetic letter–sound matches by the end of Kindergarten and yet many early Grade 1 or late Kindergarten students may not be doing much independent writing. By showing them that they can make many words by "bumping" two phonemes together and writing their letter names down in the correct sequence, teachers increase the store of known words students can spell. Imagine how helpful it is for students to have just this partial list in their list of words they can spell: *be, see, in, it, at, go, so, no, we, hi.* And if you get spellings such as "pa" for *pay* or "da" for *day*, or "li" for *lie*, it is great emergent writing! This lesson, with its fun game, is just one way to help students learn to write new words as well as get them into the habit of sounding out a word when they go to write it.

GETTING READY

First, prepare on the magnetic chalkboard a scene that looks much like the one below. Be sure to have a magnetic letter *g* (lowercase) and a magnetic letter *o* ready. Also, have a number of other magnetic letters at hand: the consonants *g, n, s, t, d, b,* and the vowels *o, i, ee,* and *e.*

HOW TO TEACH IT

Tell the students that you have a silly story that will help them learn how to make words when they know lots of letters and the sounds they make. When I tell it, I make forlorn phonemic sounds as the characters G and O traverse the meadow.

"Once upon a time in a grassy meadow, there was a little insect letter named G. He would flit from flower to flower and say in his sad little voice, 'g, g, g' [hard /g/ sound] He would sometimes fly close to the clouds and say, 'g, g, g,' and once in a while he would be really happy because a strong breeze would come along and he could just drift saying, 'g, g, g.' But G was lonely and wanted a friend.

"One day when G was sipping nectar from a flower, he saw a strange insect above him. It looked like a letter insect. It was hovering under the clouds and it was saying, 'Oh, oh, oh!' It always sounded surprised, with its mouth wide open, just like an *O*. It floated down and sat on a flower and said, 'Oh, oh, oh!' G noticed it and felt a strange excitement. He flew above the flowers and said, 'g, g, g,' and then O saw him and started towards him saying, 'Oh, oh, oh!'

"Can anyone guess what's going to happen? Well, G kept saying 'g', and O went right beside him saying 'Oh,' and before long they made a word: *g* and *oh*. The next thing you know, they both took off like a rocket! They kept saying, 'Go!' And they raced all around the meadow as happy as could be."

Next, become either the G or the O by using a magnetic letter at one side of the magnet board and getting a volunteer to take the other letter. Act out the G and O story by slowly coming closer together and saying sounds until you bump letters, with the *g* making the sound first and right after that the *o*, and then say, "Go!"

Then, invite two children to act it out, and change the letters to *s* and *o* and then *b* and *ee* or *b* and *e*. Explain that *ee* says / ē /. As each set of partners acts out the Bumping game put the word on the board.

Next day, practise "bumping" together, making words either using letter cards or magnetic letters. Ask students to think of two phoneme words and list them. Give the students time to play the Bumping game with their partners. They can use magnetic letters or just phoneme sounds. Usually, they can think of two phoneme words, but if they can't, suggest them. It's noisy, but they are learning!

Then, ask them to go to their tables and recall words made by "bumping" — I sometimes have to remind them of words we made. They can write the words down on their papers as you write them on the board. Do this together and then read the two phoneme words out loud.

REFLECTING ON THE LEARNING

Students are always amazed at how many two phoneme words they can make or think of and it is something to discuss together as you celebrate the number of words they can now write.

Do tell students that some of the words aren't in standard spelling, but in "kidwriting," words made by sounding out and writing down the sounds heard. Explain that children in Kindergarten, Grade 1, and Grade 2 do "kidwriting" while learning to spell words in standard form. It is important that they see that a word like *tie* can be represented as "ti." Questions to ask include "How many words did we make?" and "How many did you make with your partner?" Let them guess the number and help them feel proud of the quantity of words they have learned.

"We have learned to make so many new words just by bumping two phonemes together and putting down the letters for the first one and the second one. This is a clever thing to do, and when we go to write our stories, we need to remember how to do this!"

NOTES ON ASSESSMENT

Before the Lesson: For students to be ready for this lesson, they need to have a fair number of sound–symbol matches learned. This lesson is for later Kindergarten or early Grade 1 when you can be sure that most students are ready for it. However even students who know a few sound–symbol matches can benefit from this lesson. Most students recognize *o*, and with knowledge of only *s*, *n*, and *g* can make three words! Consider using "A List of Words to Assess Whether Students Can Isolate Beginning Sounds," which appears at the end of this chapter, to assess if students have the pre-skills needed for this lesson. They also need to have had some practice printing the letters as they are asked to record the two phoneme words they think of. If students have a "printing alphabet" chart for reference this will be helpful.

During the Lesson: While students are working in pairs doing their phonemic "bumping," look for these things:

- Are they able to think of two phoneme words?
- Do they position themselves so that the phonemes are in the right order?
- Are they able to put down the matching letters for phonemes?
- Do they make their letters correctly and in the right place?

After the Lesson: After they have had considerable practice with the Bumping game, get the children to spell from dictation a number of two phoneme words, such as *be, he, go, so, no, hi, see, we.* You can also test them on some non-standard words, such as *row*, looking for "ro," or *bye*, looking for "bi," and see if they are able to identify the two phonemes.

MAKING IT SIMPLER

Do Less, Go Slower: For students who have difficulty with these concepts, it is best to go slower than what is suggested in the lesson plan.

The first day, just have them work in partners to do the story of the insects ... and have them "bump" for *go*. Provide magnetic letters for them to find a *g* and an *o* and have them make *go* on the magnetic board or with letters on a table. Have them print the word *go* several times on the worksheet, perhaps "bumping" their letters each time and recording the word so that they get the idea of doing something and recording their results.

The next day, work with about six *o* words, having students make them with magnetic letters or letter cards, and then the next day, work with a number of *e* words.

Don't Bump with Partners — Just with Letters: It can be chaotic to have students "bump" their partners, and if you have a frisky class it may not be a good idea. If you have six sets of magnetic letters, you can teach this lesson to groups of students and have them bump the letters on their magnetic boards or at the magnetic chalkboard you might have. If you have paper letters, they could do the same on a flat surface like a table. You might make a blackline master out of a meadow scene (see page 79) and provide letters to re-create the story many times with different combinations of letters. Limit the number of letters that each student has because too many letters would be unwieldy.

Using Elkonin Boxes: After the initial story when you demonstrate coming together and bumping with another child, you could introduce an intermediary step to help students with the concept of positions. By sketching two Elkonin, or sound, boxes (shown below), you can help students easily see the beginning position for the first sound and the last position for the second sound. It might be visually helpful for them to do this on the board with a magnetic letter coming slowly from the left and from the right to "land" in the correct position in the Elkonin box, best placed in the board's centre.

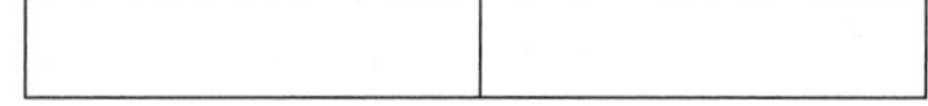

INCREASING THE CHALLENGE

- Students who are already aware of these concepts can make a list of all the two phoneme words they know and circle all those that have two letters representing one phoneme, such as *ay* for /a/ and *ee* for /e/.
- Students may work in pairs giving each other "spelling lists" of two phoneme words from lists they or you have made.
- Ask students to think of a story that has some two phoneme words in it, tell the story, and write it if they can with invented spellings. They need to circle the two phoneme words, draw a picture that goes with the story, and perhaps share it with the class.

Using Elkonin Boxes with Prompts

The lessons so far have focused on helping students learn how to segment words into separate phonemes and to some extent taught them how to blend those phonemic bits back into words. They have emphasized very simple words with only two or three phonemes, but there are lots of challenges. How do we get children using the process of hearing and recording the sounds in words to write longer words and ensure that they hear and record the sometimes elusive middle

The checkmarks on the student samples of two phoneme words indicate that the Grade 1 students can read the words they wrote in September. The students are from Pleasant Valley Elementary School, Nanaimo, British Columbia.

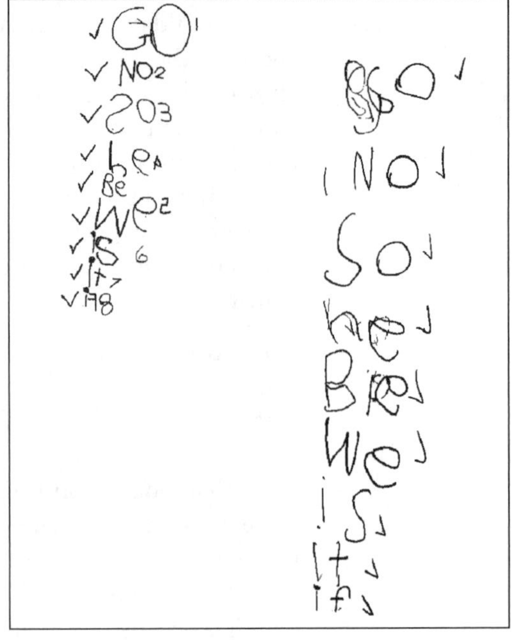

Many students know all their consonants and some of their short vowel sounds early in Grade 1, yet are not expected to spell many simple phonetic words until late in the year. Introducing this game gives students the tools to progress quickly in their emergent writing. When children write a lot, they become more proficient, so anything that gets them writing quickly is helpful.

vowel sounds in words? One way to do this is through the use of Elkonin, or sound, boxes. By playing a game with sound boxes, you can encourage students to hear all the phonemes in two, three, and four phoneme words.

The use of sound boxes is a transitional device. It helps when students are first getting accustomed to emergent spelling and stops when they are relatively proficient at isolating all the phonemes in simple words. Since writing in Writing Workshop usually has children stretching out words and putting down the sounds they hear without using Elkonin boxes, it needs to be recognized that this is just one device that may help students segment words into their phonemic parts. It does not always need to be used.

EXPLORING THE PURPOSE

For students to move into independent writing, they need to know how to solve the puzzle of writing words whose spellings they don't know. That involves stretching the words out to hear each phoneme, writing down the corresponding letters quickly, and then drafting the next word in their sentences. Students can often do this effortlessly as they are writing. Many students, however, find that an intermediary step is helpful to get them isolating words into phonemes and printing all the letter sounds they hear. Sound boxes help promote the practice of isolating words into their phonetic parts and matching the phonemes students are making in their mouths with the letters they are writing on paper. Using sound boxes with the prompts "Move it and say it" and "Say it slow and write it" has been part of Reading Recovery programs for years and is a proven way to help students learn how to spell simple phonetic words.

GETTING READY

For demonstration you will need at least three magnetic circles. You will need to reproduce sound boxes similar to those on the worksheet at the end of this lesson on the board. It is also helpful to have some simple pictures of three phoneme words, such as *cat, dog, fish, hat,* and *pot.*

Ensure that each student has three bingo markers or small cardboard circles and a copy of the worksheet "Sound Boxes." (See page 89.)

I often get students to draw sound boxes on the chalkboard or on scrap paper when they are trying to spell a word. I tell them to draw a rectangle like a chocolate bar and then cut it in half so each child gets the same-size piece, and then cut each half in half again, making four squares. It doesn't really matter if the boxes are the same size, and it is easier for them to make four boxes than three.

Magnetic circles are sold in educational supply stores but can easily be made with cardboard circles glued onto magnetic tape or magnetic paper. You can cut up many of the magnetic decals that various companies give out as advertising and glue pieces onto the back of circles or other pictures you might want to use.

HOW TO TEACH IT

Make sure that you build a bridge to past learning by talking about phonemes and discussing the Bumping game and the two phoneme words made. If possible show students a page of the two phoneme words that they made in the Bumping game. Tell them that today they will learn more about making words with two and three phonemes, and will be using sound boxes to help. Review with the students the position words *first, beginning, medial, middle,* and *end* or *last* by showing them the corresponding boxes on the board and having them locate them on their papers.

Move It and Say It

First, demonstrate how to stretch out a three phoneme word, such as *cat,* and play a game called Move It and Say It with sound boxes and magnetic circles. Tell them you are going to put your magnetic circles under the first row of boxes and that this is Home position.

Here's what it would look like:

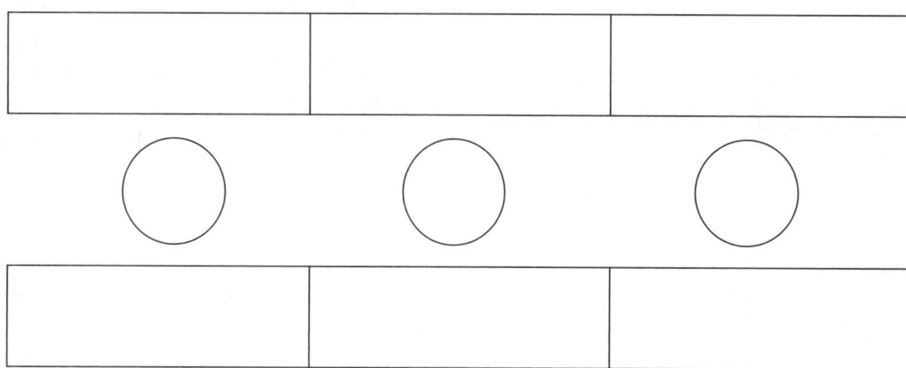

Explain that when you play Move It and Say It, you can say only one phoneme at a time and move one circle into the box above it. You could do the word *cat.* Using only your pointer finger, move the circle on the left-hand side into the box above as you say /c/, then the second middle circle into the middle box as you switch into /aa/ and then the last circle when you say /tt/. Don't pause between each phoneme, but blend into the next phoneme and move each circle into the box above it as you say it. So *cat* would be one continuous sound like this: cccccaaaaaatttttt. Then, move your three circles down to the next set of boxes and place them into Home position for the next word you're going to sound out.

Do four three phoneme words, such as *dog, cat, sun,* and *bed,* as a demonstration and then ask students to put their bingo markers or cardboard circles into Home position under the first set of boxes on their pages. Do the activity on the board while they do it at their tables.

Depending on your time and the children's interest and ability level, you could do another set of three and two phoneme words with Move It and Say It and leave the second part, Say It Slow and Write It, until the next day.

Say It Slow and Write It

First, review how to do Move It and Say It and then show students how to do the second part of the game, Say It Slow and Write It.

Put your markers into Home position and move them into sound box position while you sound out a word like *cat;* then, pick up your chalk and show them how you are now going to say it slowly and put a letter or letters in each box. Say it slowly and put *c* in the first box, then *a* in the second box, and *t* in the third box.

After a couple demonstrations with other words, ask them to do the two steps at their tables. First, they put their circles under the first row of boxes (Home position) and then use their circles to do Move It and Say It; next, they move their markers down to Home position for the next set of boxes and pick up their pencils. Now they will do Say It Slow and Write It. They stretch out the words, putting a corresponding letter or letters into each box.

After they are done ask them to read the words.

On another day you might ask students to do this more independently. You could show them pictures and ask them to do the two steps Move It and Say It and Say It Slow and Write It on their own.

REFLECTING ON THE LEARNING

Don't be too surprised if students can spell the word but find it difficult to read. This often happens!

Students are generally fairly excited about being able to spell so many words, so an emphasis on their accomplishments is appropriate. Make sure you tell them that they listened and heard ALL the sounds in the words and did not forget the vowel sounds in the middle. Many students will have been spelling these words in Writing Workshop without the medial vowel sounds. Some questions you might ask are these:

- How many phonemes did you hear in this word?
- Do you have a letter for each phoneme?
- Did you have any phonemes that were made by two letters?
- Did Move It and Say It help you know how many phonemes are in the word?
- What two things do you say when you play this game?
- Are you a better speller after learning this game?
- How will this help you when you write your stories?

NOTES ON ASSESSMENT

Before the Lesson: Students need to know the position words *beginning, middle, medial, end,* or *last,* to be successful in this lesson. They need to know the concept of matching and one-to-one correspondence so that they understand that each phoneme is matched by one letter, two letters, or maybe three letters that make one sound. They need to be aware that words begin on the left and extend toward the right. Since this lesson would take place after students were relatively sure of sound–symbol matches, this shouldn't be a problem. If children had difficulty with this lesson, however, it would helpful to review the above concepts.

Assessing students' ability to hear and record sounds can be done by using a test devised by Marie Clay. The test in *An Observation Survey* provides an indication of students' ability to hear the sounds in words. Doing Form A at the beginning of the year and then using different forms throughout the year will provide a picture of progress over time.

During the Lesson: These are questions that teachers will have in their minds as they observe students doing their sound boxes, making the sounds, and printing the letters that make the sounds.

- Are they able to isolate each phoneme?
  It is difficult to isolate each phoneme in a word and you will find students who will put the first two phonemes together, such as "ca" in *cat* or "do" in *dog*. You need to be observing and listening for this so you can go and gently ask them to think of just the beginning sound which will be the first phoneme.
- Are they doing both parts of the game?
  Some students will want to miss the Move It and Say It part and move right into spelling the word, but encourage them to do this first part. Tell them that although it seems easy with short three phoneme words, doing this will really help with longer words and that you'll give them some longer words soon! Tell them that Move It and Say It helps them find all the sounds, even the sneaky vowel sounds in the middle!
- Are they making the correct sound–symbol matches?
  Students will frequently get *b*, *p*, and *d* mixed up and these confusions need to be addressed. Vowels are often confused as well, and in this game only short-vowel words should be used.

After the Lesson: When students have had considerable practice with teacher-directed activities with sound boxes, give them a blank sheet and show them pictures of items whose names have three or four phonemes, such as *crab, slug, mitt, hand.* See if they can both move their circles accordingly and make the correct phonetic matches. If they can do correct phonetic matches for three and four phoneme words, note that on an individual assessment sheet, such as that at the end of this chapter.

MAKING IT SIMPLER

Get Them Ready for Sound Boxes: A lesson that could precede this one entails providing each student with just one sound box with four squares on a manila tag card. Using a word like *cat*, have them put a bingo chip, cardboard circle, or other marker where they hear /c/, a marker where they hear /t/, and a marker where they hear /a/. Talk about beginning, first, medial, in the middle, centre, last, at the end, and so on so that they are aware of all the position words that are helpful when thinking about sounds and letters in words.

Teach Two Phoneme Words First: If students have done the Ghost Talk lesson, they will be used to thinking about two phoneme words, and doing Move It and Say It with two phoneme words makes an easy transition. They can learn the rules of the game, putting their markers in Home position, moving the markers to each phoneme that comes out of their mouths, and penciling in their letters while they do Say It Slow and Write It.

Use Only Vowel Sounds They Know: Some students learn the short vowels quickly, but for some the task can be easier if you teach a particular vowel sound such as the short /a/ first, and then only do words that contain that vowel sound.

Do "Arm Spelling": Another strategy that sometimes helps students both segment words into phonemes and blend them together quickly is to let students use an extended arm to "place" the phonemes. Starting at the shoulder and extending down the arm, the student uses the right hand to pat the extended left arm for each phoneme said out loud. For example for *cat*, the /c/ would be patted on the shoulder of one's outstretched left arm by the right hand, the /a/ on the elbow and the /t/ on the wrist; then, using the same hand the student would sweep down the left arm, putting all the sounds together to say *cat* quickly. This kinesthetic way to segment and blend phonemes in words can supplement the Move It and Say It approach.

INCREASING THE CHALLENGE

- When you have a variety of two, three, and four phoneme words, students don't have a visual telling them how many phonemes are in the word. You may give them a four phoneme sheet and have them start in Home position with all four markers, but when they get a word like *at* they will use only two markers. Follow a two phoneme word with *crab*, for example, and they have to use four markers.
- Digraphs are two letters that represent one phoneme. Adding words that contain the digraphs *sh*, *th*, or *ch* helps to make the task more challenging. Vowel combinations, such as *ee* and *ai*, will also increase the challenge.

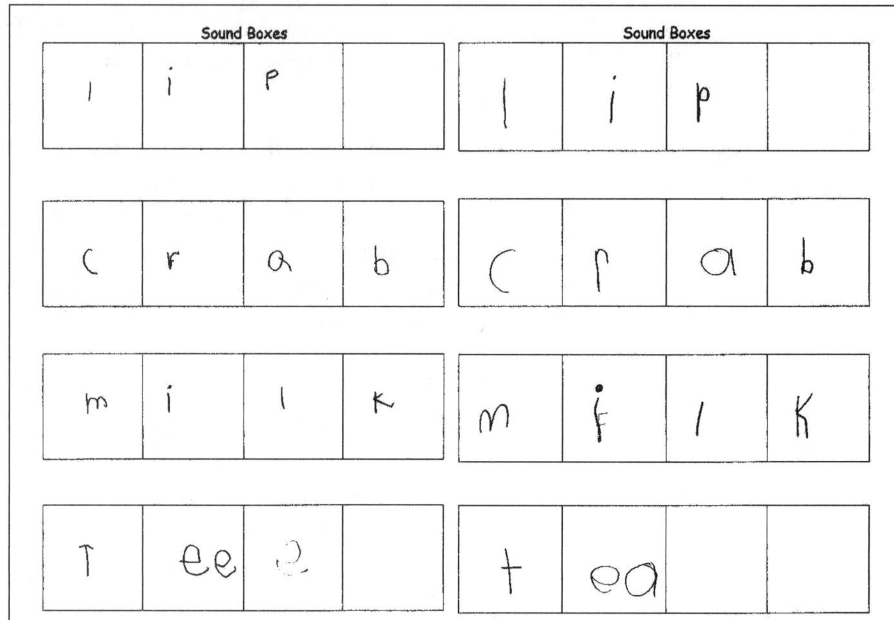

The sheets below were completed by Grade 2 students from Pleasant Valley Elementary School, Nanaimo, British Columbia, in September.

This chapter will help students obtain the Basic Tools to advance quickly in their independent writing. When students have considerable practice listening for all the phonemes in a word, they will usually be better able to do successful phonetic spelling "on the fly,"or as they are writing. Having explored, both through writing and reading, numerous words that have vowel sounds in the middle and consonant blends at the beginning and end, they will be prepared to listen for those sounds in words they are spelling in independent writing. As students practise using sound boxes and think of "bumping" words, their spellings will evolve from "kidwriting," the invented spellings that students do as they write words they have stretched out phonetically, to something more standard in appearance.

Checklist for Phonemic Skills

Name ______________________________

1 unable to do the task
2 attempts the task with minimal ability
3 demonstrates average ability with a distinct need for further practice
4 demonstrates good ability that meets the age-appropriate standard for the task

Skill *Dates:*					*Comments:*
Can give examples of a phoneme, a word, and a sentence					
Can isolate the beginning sound in a list of words beginning with consonant sounds					
Can isolate the ending sound in a list of words ending with consonant sounds					
Can isolate and count the phonemes in a three phoneme word, e.g., c a t					
Can isolate and count the phonemes in a four-letter word, e.g., s l a p					
Can match the phonemes with a letter that makes that sound (not necessarily the correct letter) in a list of two phoneme words					
Can match the phonemes with the matching letter or letter cluster in a list of three and four phoneme words					
Can match the phonemes heard with the matching letter symbol in a dictated simple sentence					
Can identify a word that rhymes with a given word					
Can identify words that rhyme in a list of four words, one of which does not rhyme with the others					

A List of Words to Assess Whether Students Can Isolate Beginning Sounds

Student's Name ______________________________ Date ____

Ask the student to repeat the word after you, check the accuracy, and then ask if the student can make the beginning sound of the word. As a model, do these words together: *sand, hello, mine.*

Word	*Says It Correctly*	*Isolates Beg. Sound*	*Word*	*Says It Correctly*	*Isolates Beg. Sound*
apple			card		
nest			deep		
happy			end		
baby			gate		
fire			lips		
kick			rooster		
jump			queen		
pot			often		
windy			money		
under			yarn		
snake			zip		
top			vase		
into			shut		

Phonemes that need to be worked on:

____

____

Beginning sounds the student has trouble isolating:

____

____

Sound Boxes

Ghost Talk — Wordy

5

Learning How to Spell

Teaching reading and writing, especially at the beginning stages, go together. It is difficult to talk about Basic Tools for beginning writers without referring to the way in which reading is taught. As students read their first simple pattern books, they learn to read a basic sight vocabulary and teachers usually devote some part of their reading lessons to teaching students how to write some of the simple words they are learning to read. That means some of the following lessons will take place around the guided reading table with students who come prepared with pencil and paper or little chalkboards.

Many primary classrooms have Word Walls, where sight words are posted on a wall under the alphabet letter each word begins with so that students can look at the wall when they need to spell a word. Numerous books, some listed in Recommended Resources, offer activities that teachers can use with Word Walls to help students learn how to spell.

I have always had a Word Wall and used it; however, I believe that when we want children to write, they need to spend their time thinking about what they need to say. Frequently looking up at a Word Wall or even worse, getting out of their seats to go and look at a Word Wall, is distracting to the thinking process. Many teachers provide a reference chart of some basic hard-to-spell words that students can paste into the front of their writing books or have at their desks as a reference, and I believe this is less distracting. At the end of this chapter a list titled "Harder to Spell High-Frequency Words" appears for your use with beginning writers.

As primary teachers, we want several things for our students:

- to be fearless spellers, finding no word too difficult to stretch out and spell: with lots of phonemic practice behind them, students can make good phonetic spellings of many words.
- to know how to spell many simple sight words without having to think about their individual sounds: if they think more about chunks than individual phonemes, students who can spell a word like *night* will also be able to spell *light* and *right* — part of the same "word family."
- to know some simple spelling rules, such as "When two vowels go walking the first one does the talking and says its own name" (even though this rule doesn't work for all long vowel words)

- to develop a great visual memory which comes as they are exposed to lots of print

There are many ways of describing that group of words commonly found in most English sentences, for example, ***the*****,** ***they*****,** ***are*****,** ***like*****,** ***what*****,** ***with*****, and** ***for*****. They are often referred to as basic sight vocabulary, anchor words, or even "popcorn" words because they pop up so often. These terms will be used interchangeably in the following lessons.**

Students also learn how to spell by the act of writing a lot of words, so it is important to provide opportunities for students to write often, in all subject areas.

When I walk into a Grade 2 classroom and see short three- and four-letter phonetic words on the board as part of a spelling list, I always wonder why such simple words are still difficult for students — it is their third year of writing. Sometimes, I believe, teachers stick to a curriculum that teaches a majority of children what they already know. Students are best served by teachers who look carefully at their writing, celebrate the spelling knowledge they demonstrate, and make sure they teach them the next step in the process rather than slavishly following a given spelling program.

The following lessons may provide an efficient way for students to learn to spell basic sight words and can, I believe, take the place of a formal spelling program.

Read It! Write It!

Students can often print their names although they may not be able to identify every letter. Their names have meaning, they can "make" their names, and they can read them! When students first learn to read they are usually given a simple pattern book where a sentence frame is repeated on each page with a picture that tells what item the last word or words on the page will be. For example, each page of a book may begin with the frame *I like to eat.* On one page there will be an apple, on another a banana, and perhaps a pear on the third page to create a story that reads: *I like to eat an apple, I like to eat a banana, I like to eat a pear.* Simple pattern books like this teach children to follow from left to right as they read, to match one word on the page to a word out of their mouths, and to know a basic sight vocabulary that they can both read and write. The two processes complement each other. When students can write *I like to eat* from memory, they can usually read the words as well. Of course, you may teach the students to write the sentence frame *I like to* on Monday, and they may have forgotten it by Wednesday! Students need numerous exposures to a word in print, both reading and writing it, before it becomes theirs in long-term memory.

While students are at the guided reading group, the rest of the class is engaged in other literacy activities. What has worked best for me is to have all the students working on a writing task related to a science, social, or seasonal theme, for example, writing out a set of four facts about whales and adding an illustration. They would do this content writing after rehearsing ideas with a partner. When finished writing, they could go to a quiet literacy centre of their choice.

Many primary teachers teach reading in guided reading groups, where students are at a similar developmental level. The instruction is challenging in that there will be new things for students to learn, but not frustrating as there will be much that is familiar and easy. In this instructional zone, with good teaching and small numbers of students, students have an excellent chance to experience success and receive positive feedback about their progress. It is generally understood that some part of that lesson will be devoted to word study and spelling of the simple vocabulary students are reading. Although you can teach students in a large group using these same strategies, the following lesson ideas have been tailored to work well with a group of six or fewer children sitting around a table.

EXPLORING THE PURPOSE

When students learn to read and write simple words together, both skills are strengthened. Children will remember those words they have made with magnetic letters or paper and pencil while they read and will remember their reading while they write.

Here, you will see some of the strategies for learning sight words during a guided reading lesson. They will help children learn words that they do not need to segment into isolated phonemes in order to spell. Many of the words that pop up often in their reading are not phonetically standard short-vowel words, but words such as *the*, *one*, and *to*. They must be learned by sight.

Six classroom sets of magnetic letters are essential tools for beginning readers and writers. I keep them in one of the storage boxes with lots of little drawers so that each drawer has one or two letters. I can easily put out the letters needed for the lesson and students put the letters away by matching them with the letters glued to the front of each drawer.

Magnetic boards are simply round stove-burner covers and are easily available at dollar stores. Small cookie sheets work well too, but the large stove-burner covers stack, are colourful and bright, and are much cheaper!

GETTING READY

I like to have children working at a round table but have seen many classrooms where students in a group of six or fewer sit on the floor in a semi-circle. Because I want students to shift between identical little books, paper and pencil, and magnetic boards, I find the table easiest.

No matter what setting you choose, you will need paper and pencil for each student and a magnetic board with the letters of the word or words you want them to spell in random order at the top of the board. You will also need chalkboard or whiteboard space for demonstration, and chalk or erasable marker.

HOW TO TEACH IT

I usually prefer to do my word work before a lesson so that when students go to read their little books, they have a better chance of reading successfully; I do agree, though, that having the students read the little book first will introduce the words and ideas in a concrete, meaningful way. I will use *Fruits I Like* for this lesson on teaching students to write "I like to eat ..."

Invite students to tell you what fruits they like to eat and write many of their sentences on the board. Say something like, "Mary says, 'I like to eat an orange'" and then write, *I like to eat an orange* on the board. Perhaps put Mary's name in small letters beside the sentence. As students read these sentences back, they gain lots of exposure to the words in print and will be very pleased to see their names.

Have the magnetic letters for *I like to eat* on the board all tight together. The first task is for the students to help you with separating the mass of letters into words by making spaces. They love to say "I like to eat" really fast as if it was one word. At this beginning stage, they need to recognize the singleness of each word and how important it is to make spaces between them.

Since most students will know *I* and *to*, focus on the words *like* and *eat*, following this process to give students a chance to play with each word:

1. You write the word slowly on the board, talking about the letters and how they are made. As you do this, students watch and listen.
2. Students write the word on their papers while you write it on the board, talking about letter formation as you go.
3. They write it again on their papers, using the model on the chalkboard but without your help; you assist where necessary.
4. They put their papers down and find the letters to make the word with their magnetic letters in the centre of their boards.
5. You make the word with your magnetic letters and ask them to check if it is right.
6. Students make a windstorm to mix up their letters.
7. Students then rearrange letters to see if they can make the word again without looking at the reference word on the board.
8. Ask them to check the board and make the word again.

9. Students see if they can make the word with pencil and paper again without looking at the board. They could make it more than once, first slowly and then quickly — you want a fast response.

Follow this procedure for both *like* and *eat.*

Then, model printing the sentence frame *I like to eat …*, emphasizing spaces and letter formation, and have students write it on their papers. They would also make the sentence with their magnetic boards.

Last, have them write *I like to eat* from memory on a sentence strip, a piece of paper, or a page in their notebooks, and you could fill in the last two words, for example *red apples*, with some talk of them making the first letter of the name of the fruit they like. They could then draw pictures of their fruit.

Post-lesson suggestions

Students need to know that "kidwriting," where they stretch words out and write down the phonemes in words that don't have standard spellings, is always acceptable good practice, but there are words you will expect to see written in standard English. For example, when you know that students have been taught and given much practice writing *like* or *eat* with proper spellings, begin to expect that those words will not appear as "lik" or "et" in their Writing Workshop work.

- Make sure that you put the words *like, to,* and *eat* on flashcards.
- Next day, as a review, ask students to spell these words.
- Incorporate the words into their spelling literacy centres for "playtime."
- Put the words on the Word Wall for use in the many spelling games that can be played with Word Wall words.
- Provide opportunities for students to use these words in their informal writing, such as drafting a shopping list or menu ideas at the home centre,
- Encourage students to spell the words correctly in Writing Workshop.

REFLECTING ON THE LEARNING

After some guided practice, you will want to encourage students to make the word independently and to see if they were accurate by looking at the model and comparing their word to it. Both of these behaviors need to be reinforced by positive comments. Some of the questions and prompts that will encourage these behaviors are as follows:

- What word did you make? Can you read it to me?
- Did you make this word correctly? How do you know?
- Can you find the word in the story on the board? What does it say?
- Can you make the word on your own? How can you check to make sure it is right?
- What words did you learn to spell today? Where will you get a chance to write them in the next little while?

NOTES ON ASSESSMENT

Many students will know how to write *like* and *eat* before this lesson and if they do, you need to check whether they can read at this level as well. If they are having difficulty with that, this lesson's reading content will be useful to them and they will enjoy being able to follow the lesson easily.

Before the Lesson: Students do not need to know all letter names and sounds before doing this lesson, although of course it is helpful. Some students will learn that *L* is the letter that *like* starts with and will learn their alphabet sounds and letters from concrete words that they can read and make. It is expected that this beginning Grade 1 or later Kindergarten lesson in formal reading would be done with students who have had lots of informal reading experience with Morning Message, Big Books read together, songs and poems on charts, as well as informal reading of pattern books at independent reading time. Students will need to be able to follow directions and have the necessary focus to follow a model in making a word.

Check to see if students can spell *I like to eat* before the lesson. If they can do so easily and read at this level as well, they probably don't need this!

During the Lesson: When observing a student consider the following questions: Is the student able to

- print the word to look like the model that is demonstrated?
- make the word with magnetic letters using a reference word as a model?
- rearrange the mixed-up letters to create the word on the magnetic board quickly?
- make the word on the magnetic board accurately without referencing the model?
- create the sentence or sentence frame with proper spacing and letter formation?
- benefit from repeated practice?

After the Lesson: With many opportunities beyond this lesson to practise both reading the words in meaningful print and making the words in sessions with magnetic letters and paper and pencil, the student can be tested on ability to both read and write the words *I, like, to,* and *eat* in isolation.

MAKING IT SIMPLER

Although a definition of a guided reading group suggests that every child in the group is at the same instructional level, there will be differentiated abilities within every group. Some students will need challenges and some will need extra help even within a small group. Since most teachers find that three is the maximum number of guided reading groups they can accommodate easily, they need to be prepared both to challenge some students and somewhat simplify the lesson for others.

One Word Only: Students who learn more slowly than others need to have more repetition and will benefit from having only one word such as *like* to focus on in the lesson. Choose either *like* or *eat* to focus on during the lesson rather than both. Spend more practice time with helping the students write the word hand over hand to get the letter formation down pat. If possible, provide little chalkboards instead of paper and pencil so they can write the word larger.

Give the Beginning Letter: As an intermediary step with students who have difficulty remembering, you can prompt them to make the word *like* by themselves but give them the *l* or even the *l* and *e*; ask them to put in the letters that go in the middle. You can create a puzzle for them that looks like this: l_ _ e. Then go to _ _ _e and finally to _ _ _ _. This step will help them think about all the letters in the word.

Emphasize the Shape of the Word: Sometimes it helps to talk about the shape of the whole word. If you describe how *like* starts off tall and then has a dip, is tall again and then has a dip at the end, and draw a shape around it, this will help students visualize the word and spell it.

INCREASING THE CHALLENGE

In Writing Workshop, it is advisable to discourage list stories, or stories with the same beginning sentence frame. However, while students are learning to read and write basic sight words, these sentence frame stories are useful for practice.

- You may ask students who can easily write *I like to eat* to create list stories about four or five things they enjoy eating. They can do this quietly while you are practising the creation of a word with the rest of the students. Their stories might be something like this: *I like to eat raisins, I like to eat carrots, and I like to eat an ice-cream cone.* They could write in little blank booklets while enjoying the reading practice that is part of this lesson.

Working with Word Families — The Power of Onset and Rime

It is important for students to listen to and sing rhymes, make up rhyming couplets, and manipulate sounds to make words that rhyme with a given word. When primary teachers move from students listening to writing, it is time to explain that rhyming words that end with the same group of letters are put together in *word families.* In each of these words that rhyme, there is a beginning sound called an *onset* and a following chunk called a *rime.* Students need to understand that rimes always look the same, but the letter combinations that create rhymes — for example, *dine* and *sign* — may differ.

As students learn to read and spell, it is more efficient for them to recognize and print chunks of words rather than always think of the individual phonemes that make up each word. In this way they can read and write faster. They learn that *-at* is a chunk and that *fat, bat, rat,* and *sat* are all part of this word family. Similarly, *-ing* and *-ike* are rimes.

Word families are important so I always teach the common word families that link to text students are learning to read. However, they do not need extensive practice with every word family. Once students know how to identify common word families and chunks in words and are using these processes in their independent reading and spelling, the teaching of word families can be more incidental than deliberate.

EXPLORING THE PURPOSE

Teaching students word families means that if they know how to spell a word like *fine,* they can also spell *dine, mine, pine,* and *line.* They thereby gain many opportunities to increase their store of correctly spelled words. Of course, they may spell *sign* as *sine* and make some logical errors, but introducing word families is still a useful way to expand their ability to spell. When students learn to identify the rime of a word such as *dine,* they can read words that are part of that word family; however, this doesn't happen quickly for most children. Teaching students to read and write words as part of word families will help them become better spellers and readers.

GETTING READY

This simple lesson uses one strategy to help students learn about word families. It can be done with the whole group or in a group of six students. It is best done with students sitting in a semi-circle or at a table with small chalkboards, socks or erasers, and chalk. You may use magnetic letters at the chalkboard or just do the "finger slide" as the lesson illustrates. If you do the lesson in a small group, you may want to provide laminated cards showing a teeter-totter–style slide. Students can place letters that represent onsets onto a slide where they land on the beginning of the rime, at the bottom of the slide.

Consider a student stuck on reading the word *hike*. If you know the word *like* is familiar, you could say: "Does this word look like a word you know?" Put your finger over the first letter and ask, "Do you know another word that has letters like this chunk?" Getting students faced with a word they can't read to think of word family chunks as clues is very helpful.

HOW TO TEACH IT

Once students have learned and used a sight word for several days, they are ready to learn about the word families associated with that word. I always choose words that students are learning to read and write in their text experiences. The links between reading and writing should be strong and reinforce each other, so my choice of word family doesn't come from a "program," but rather from the words they are reading daily. The lesson below focuses on the word *like.*

If teaching this lesson, you would print the word *like* on the board and talk about how you and the students have used it in writing and reading in order to make sure that all students understand the context of how to use the word. Then, tell them that they are going to learn how knowing the spelling of one word can help them read and write a family of words, in this case, the *-ike* family.

Slowly tell a brief story, such as the one on page 97, and ask students to listen for all the words that rhyme. List the words and then tell them you are going to show them a way to spell these words easily. Ask them to tell you what letters are the same in each word. Explain that *-ike* is a rime and that when you change the beginning letter (or two), which is called the onset, you have a new word.

I recommend making word families out of words that are not simple three- or four-letter phonetic words, such as *sat, fat, tin, bin*. These words are easily spelled with a simple hearing and recording of sounds, while words with a silent *e* or long vowel made by two vowels, such as *ai* or *oa*, are often spelled accurately by remembering the word family chunk.

"Mike has a bike that isn't much good on a hike. What does he like? Mike says, 'Not a trike! I want a mountain bike!'"

Next, tell them you are going to play a little game and find some words that are part of the *-ike* family and were part of the story. Sketch a slide on the board.

The slide needn't have so much detail as shown here. It can also be represented more like a teeter-totter, with the rime weighing down one end of the board and onsets at the high end.

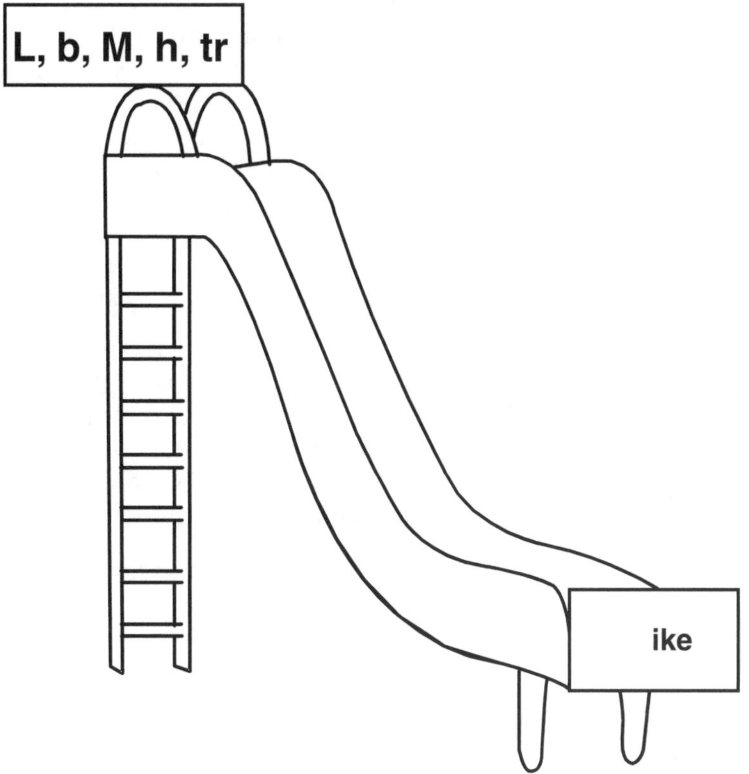

The story is about how each little onset rolls down the slide and lands in front of the *-ike* rime to create a new word. Each word is a member of the *-ike* family. As you show each letter going down the slide, the students make the beginning sound throughout the letter's journey. When it lands in front of *-ike*, they then say the word. Print each word on the board, and ask the students to read it together. It's recommended that you make about four or five words.

Most students will not remember how to spell these words after a single lesson. Review by including the words in a spelling literacy centre, such as the teacher–students centre outlined in Chapter 3, encouraging their spelling in independent writing, and using them in re-creating readable text, such as rhymes. Ask the students to spell them during "sponge" activities, as a way out the door, or in a weekly spelling review. Such reinforcement will help students remember these spellings.

The students then re-create the story for themselves. They either have their chalk or magnetic letters slide. They first pretend to stick the letter into the chalk's memory and then deposit it by having the chalk "unlock" the memory; they write the letter in front of *-ike* after it completes its journey down the slide. After they have slid all the letters down the slide and read each new word at the bottom, they rub everything off or put their laminated slides away.

Ask them to write the words from memory and assist as necessary. At the end they should have made such words as *like, bike, Mike, hike,* and *trike.*

These words would then go either on the Word Wall or on a word family chart, becoming "spelling" words to be reviewed and spelled often.

REFLECTING ON THE LEARNING

Helping students understand that they can create a whole list of words from knowing the word family of familiar words is powerful. You might say something like the following:

"This morning you knew how to spell *like* and now you know how to spell *bike, hike, trike,* and *Mike,* all because you know how a word family works. This is important learning!"

Some questions to ask are these:

- Can you show me what part of the word makes the rime? How many letters is it? Is it the same in all the words?
- How many new words did we make?
- Can you read these words?
- Can you write these words?
- If I tell you that this word is *mine* [print it for them] how would you make *dine*? Write it for me. How would you make *pine*? What is the rhyming word family in this word?

NOTES ON ASSESSMENT

Before the Lesson: This lesson should be done with a known word or words that students have had lots of experience with in terms of reading and writing. Checking to make sure that students can recognize or sound out at least one of the words in the word family you are discussing is useful.

Students should know the concepts of rhyming words and beginning sounds before this lesson.

During the Lesson: While students are re-creating a word-family story with their chalkboards, you can determine if they can make the letter sounds that match the onsets and whether they can read the new word they have made by supplying a new onset to the rime *-ike.* Carry a little chalkboard with you and ask a student to quickly make one of the words for you while you cover up the words on his or her page. This will help you determine whether the student remembers the onset or can use new knowledge about onset and rime to combine the two to make an unfamiliar word.

After the Lesson: Checking to see if students understand the process is important. Can students transfer the knowledge they have learned about one word family to another word family? If you give them a known word, perhaps *ride,* can they make *side* or *tide*?

Can they spell the words from memory? Check a few days after the lesson and see if they have retained their learning. If you give them the known word *like,* can they spell *hike*?

Can they recognize words that have the same rime as the known word? For example, if you put the word *hike* on the board and tell them it is like a word they know, can they read it? Can they give you a word that rhymes with it?

Another assessment of their ability is to ask them to make a word that rhymes with a known word, but begins with a different beginning sound. For example, you might say: "Spell the word *slug* that rhymes with *bug.* Spell the word *right* that rhymes with *light.*"

MAKING IT SIMPLER

Include Move It and Say It: A step to take before you play the game where the letter goes down the slide is to do Move It and Say It, as explained in Chapter 4. Using sound boxes (only three sounds for *like*—you would put *k* and the ending *e* in the same box), students would have both the phonetic clues and the visual memory of the *-ike* family to help them remember the rime.

Choose a Simpler Word Family: Word family chunks are good ways to help students write words that have a silent *e* ending or words with long-vowel sounds, such as *tail* and *beach*, rather than the simplest phonetic short-vowel words, such as *cat*, *dog*, and *pin*; however, beginning with simpler word families will help some students learn the concept with more success.

INCREASING THE CHALLENGE

- Give students a familiar word and ask them to make a list of word family words from that word. For example, give them the word *pen*, *ride*, or *see*.
- When they have demonstrated they can write their list of words, ask them to create a little story that uses at least three of these words.

Creating a Weekly Spelling List

In most Grade 1 classrooms I have been in, there has been evidence of some kind of formal spelling program, but as this book presents, there are many opportunities for informal spelling practice: Morning Message, Writing Workshop, interactive writing, writing at centres, learning Move It and Say It, and learning how to spell words students are reading.

Some teachers supplement these spelling practices with a list of words to spell from the Word Wall, a sight word list such as the Dolch list of common words, or phonetically based spelling programs. There are many different approaches to learning how to write words accurately, including not having any formal spelling program at all. Students learn to spell as they write, and in my observation, students who do a lot of writing in a Writing Workshop–type environment generally learn to spell more quickly than others who write less.

Certain key beliefs have led me to create the text-based spelling ideas in the following lesson.

- Young students benefit most from concrete language experiences. I believe that reading is best taught with little books using ordinary language rather than with phonetic lists of words or words in isolation.
- If teachers can give students concrete experiences, such as holding artifacts, seeing visuals about animals or places they are going to read about, and exploring through guided imagery the sensory details of items, places, and feelings they are going to encounter in text, these experiences will make reading more comprehensible.
- Students should learn to spell words they have seen often in meaningful print, such as in the books they read, the songs they sing, or the poems and chants they listen to, repeat, and talk about.
- Students should write about their own realities: their personal stories, their responses to literature, and their individual observations.
- When reading and writing experiences are linked, learning in both areas is reinforced.

Although there may be formal expectations that students up to Grade 3 do not have homework, in some school communities, sending home a weekly spelling list for study is a popular practice, as is a Home Reading program. I found this even with the families of Grade 1 students. School practices where children brought home tasks to do with parents were valued.

Also, in my experience, students do not need to learn spelling words in a strict hierarchical order where they first learn simple short-vowel words and then progress to words with a final *e*, and then to words with more complex vowel patterns. Of course, that is within reason! Students will not learn to spell *stupendous* before they learn to spell *sat*. Grade 1 teachers, however, often find students know how to spell *Superman* or *Pokemon* before they can spell *sat*. For this reason I don't slavishly follow a set of phonetic steps in introducing new words, but do progress in a general way from simple to more complex.

EXPLORING THE PURPOSE

The lesson ideas below are based on bringing together spelling ideas already presented in the book around a simple piece of text, such as a poem. There are considerable benefits to this approach. Curriculum demands on early primary teachers are many; knowing that, you have to fit in poetry experiences with the stories, formal reading, writing, and Basic Tools lessons that all students need. This lesson presents a poem or song which children might learn to chant or read chorally as well as sing; it becomes the basis of a list of six to eight words that become the spelling focus of the week.

The words are learned in the context of a meaningful piece of text, often related to a relevant seasonal or science theme that you will refer to over time. With careful choices, you can find texts with words that are simple for your students struggling with spelling as well as a few more difficult words, allowing for the differentiated learning abilities in your class. Choosing commonly used words means that students will be able to demonstrate their spelling skills during times of the day when these words are part of their independent writing experiences.

GETTING READY

To make a poem easy to read and large without a lot of effort, use the Comic Sans font of your computer, create the poem in landscape on Page Setup, use the largest font size that works for the length of your lines (probably 36) and print on letter-size paper. Then, enlarge on a photocopier to your largest paper size, usually 11 by 17. If you laminate this, it can last for many years. Using an overhead projector makes this an easy task as well, but you may not be able to display the poem over the course of the week for the students to view often.

The poem needs to be displayed in large print where everyone can see it easily. Use as many sticky notes as words you want to focus on — I would have six. Have a blank piece of chart paper ready and a blank piece of paper for each child. If possible, have magnetic circles for Move It and Say It available. You will also need chalkboard space for demonstrations. For this lesson I will use this traditional children's song:

Twinkle, Twinkle little star,
How I wonder what you are,
Up above the world so high,
Like a diamond in the sky,
Twinkle, Twinkle little star,
How I wonder what you are.

HOW TO TEACH IT

This lesson is taught over four days, with about 10 to 15 minutes devoted to it each day. On the last day is a spelling test, or challenge.

Begin by singing the song, using a pointer to point at the words as the students join you. Then, you and the students may say the words as you point at them or group the words in fluent phrases. Next, you could have children point at the words as you all sing or chant, have boys sing one line and girls the next line, or perhaps do actions or use clapping to make the song enjoyable. Each day, begin the lesson with a review of the song or poem, having fun singing, chanting, or doing a choral reading of the selection.

Next, put sticky notes over six key words. In this lesson the words will be *little, star, you, are, how,* and *sky.* You may also want to include two Challenge words, perhaps *above* and *wonder,* but don't put sticky notes on these; they will be for those students who want to take the Spelling Challenge on Friday and are willing to learn the words on their own.

You may collect their papers, summarize what they have done during this lesson, and continue with work on the words the next day.

With the class, read the song again and determine which word will be under the first sticky note. Prompt students to write on their papers the way they think it might be spelled, asking them to stretch out their sounds and think about what they remembered. After stopping at each sticky note, unveil the word and tell them to write it again, the proper way. This is not a test, but provides opportunities for students to exercise their visual memory and think about hearing and recording sounds in words.

Then, ask them to fold their papers in half three times — twice from the bottom and once across — to make eight squares. Tell them to turn to the clean sides of their papers, where they will study each word.

Since digging out bingo markers or cardboard circles for Move It and Say It can be a hassle, after they have had lots of experience with the real items, I teach students to use their fingers to move imaginary markers; however, I use magnetic markers on the board as I demonstrate. I ask them to outline a rectangular box in the middle of their square, cut it in half with a pencil, and then cut each half in half again to make four relatively equal-sized boxes.

The word determines the kinds of activities the class might do. If the word has a phonetic spelling such as in *wish*, you might make sound boxes and use fingers to Move It and Say It and then Say It Slow and Write It. If it is part of a relatively familiar word family such as *like*, you can create a list of words that rhyme with the word, using a slide on the chalkboard to reinforce the rime students should know. If it contains two syllables you can clap out the word to determine how many vowel sounds you will be dealing with. This would work for the word *wonder*. If it contains a little word or a chunk that students know, build around the known word or chunk. If it has an irregular spelling, have students practise visualizing it and writing it from memory. It is a good idea to do more than one thing with the word in order to think about it thoroughly.

Below is an example of teacher talk and student practice activities through the words *little* and *star*:

A common practice for determining the number of syllables in a word is to clap out the word and listen to how many beats or syllables it has. Words need not be split into syllables with complete accuracy, but students need to know that each syllable contains one vowel sound, although not necessarily one vowel. I tell them that each syllable is like a little bed for a vowel sound, and they have to be good parents and check to see that each little vowel is in bed when you spell. A silly story, but it works!

For *little*:

"The word we are going to learn about is *little*. Let's clap it and see how many beats or syllables are in it." [Clap.] "Make a little bed for each part of the word, and remember we have to put a vowel sound in that bed." [Draw a diagram like this on the board. ______ ______]

"Let's think of the first chunk, which is *lit*. It has our little word *it* in it. When I give the signal, spell it out loud. Let's put that part of the word in the first bed. Does this bed have a vowel sound? Put your thumb up if you see it. What is the vowel sound?

"Now, let's think about the last chunk, *-tle*. What sounds do you hear? Let's all make the letters in the air with our pointer fingers. Yes, it's a *t* and an *l* and a bit of a surprise — a silent *e* on the end. That little bed needed a vowel! Put it in the second bed. Now read your word.

"*Little* has two hard things to remember. It has two *t*'s in the middle and a silent *e* on the end. Cover up your little beds and write *little*, remembering the two special things about it. Did you write it correctly? Now write it again fast. Turn to your partner and tell them the two special things to remember about spelling *little*. Write it one more time on your paper."

For *star*:

"This word is part of the *-ar* family. When you hear the sound /ar/ in a word it is usually made by the two letters *ar*. Let's make a sound box and see how many phonemes are in *star*. Let's Move It and Say It together. S...t....ar.... How many phonemes? Yes, three. Remember that the phoneme /ar/ is made with two letters, an *a* and an *r*. Now Say It Slow and Write It. Did you write it like this? [Put the word on the board.]

"Let's think of some of the word family words for *star*. What is this word?" [Write *far*.] "Whisper it when I give the signal. Now this word" [Write *bar* on the board and ask them to whisper it when you give the signal], "and this word *tar*. That is sticky black goop!

"Now I'm going to rub these words off the board. The hard part of these words is that /ar/ is made with two letters, *a* and *r*. Now write *star*, *far*, *tar*, and *bar*. When you are done, raise your hand and I'll write them back on the board so you can check. Write the two letters that make the sound /ar/ on your partners' hands and partners, you whisper the letters back to the person who made them on your hands."

Continue with the other words.

Summarize the lesson to this point and continue on Day 3. The sheet that the students prepared can go home with them and become their practice sheet for studying.

The next practice activity that students can do is "Spelling Sheet," a blackline master following this lesson. Place the six or eight words on the board and have the students copy them onto their sheets. The activities are fairly explanatory: print and circle the word, chunk the word and say it, print it quickly, and cover your work and test yourself. Although you may have to do it with the students for the first few times, soon this activity can be done independently.

Students then go to their individual chalkboards where they practise writing each word numerous times. They can partner up and give each other "spelling tests" as practice.

On the last day dictate the words to them as a spelling test, making sure that you use each word in the line of the song, so that they have the context.

REFLECTING ON THE LEARNING

Asking students questions such as these will help them think about their learning:

- Are you able to spell this word without looking at a model?
- Do you know the hard part or something to remember in this word?
- Were you able to spell this word last week? Can you spell it now?
- What strategies did you use to help spell this word?

For those students who cannot put down beginning sounds and at least one other sound while attempting to spell a word, you need to create an alternative activity while you do the spelling test with the rest of the group. These students will probably be unable to spell the words on the test. Rather than have them become frustrated and discouraged, let them do something like work on beginning sounds on a computer program. They can participate in the rest of the program, though, because it is supported throughout with teacher responses and answers and examples on the board.

NOTES ON ASSESSMENT

Before the Lesson: This kind of spelling list is suitable for students when they can spell a number of basic sight words, have begun to read, and have done several lessons on Move It and Say It and Say It Slow and Write It. Knowing your students is crucial in choosing the words in your word list.

Having students attempt to spell the focus words on their own the first day is where you can assess their spelling potential. Most students will probably have one or two letters of each word correct and the beginning sound. This would indicate that the words are appropriate.

During the Lesson: There are many times during the students' word work where they have to indicate that they can spell on paper or aloud, find the missing letters in a word, match phonemes to letters or letter clusters, and give their partners or you some information that demonstrates they have the skills to determine how to spell a word. You need to monitor their understanding by checking how well they follow directions and give appropriate responses, and, most of all, if they can spell the word on their own after much time looking at it, talking about it, and taking it apart. If you sense that they have difficulty with this task, make sure you schedule a special "lesson" just before the spelling test on the last day to ensure that they will be successful; also, consider creating a simpler list for these students.

After the Lesson: The test given on the final day of the lessons (usually on Friday) will give you a formal assessment of their ability to spell and scores should be noted weekly in an assessment record. However, long-term memory for spelling is what really counts. It is necessary to review these words continuously and test students on the same words again a few weeks after the initial test. These results will provide a more accurate assessment. It is also important to note if they transfer these correct spellings to their independent writing work.

MAKING IT SIMPLER

Easiest to Hardest: If your first four spelling words are the easiest, you can limit your students who struggle with spelling to a four-word spelling list, and give them a score out of 4. In this way, although they go through the practice for the next two words, the changed expectations ensure that they have a good chance of being successful.

An Extra Lesson before the Test: One strategy that can help students to do well in their spelling tests is to give those few students who struggle a special lesson for 5 to 10 minutes before the test. Review the words, have them spell them on the magnetic board with magnetic letters, and discuss memory tricks. You might find time to do this while other students do independent reading. Overall performance can be enhanced by striving to make sure that these students have every opportunity to spell at least four words correctly on their tests. A buddy can sometimes be the teacher for this short review.

Provide a Buddy Tutor: Not all students have parents available to help them study for their spelling tests, and providing these students with buddies, older students from another class, is a big help. With their buddies, your students can write the word a number of times, fill in the blanks as the buddies make up spelling puzzles for each word — for example, for *little* a buddy might write l__ __ __ l e — make the word with magnetic letters, and create rhyming words with the focus word. It is important to train the buddies so that they do more than just test and mark words spelled incorrectly. Ten minutes with a buddy during the week and a 10-minute final lesson before the spelling test will usually ensure that students who do not have serious learning problems can spell at least four of the words correctly.

Provide Intermediate Steps: Here are some other activities that students can do to learn to spell their words.

- Do spelling cloze by printing the words with blanks where letters need to go. Write the poem or other text and put in blanks to represent missing letters. For example, you could write Twinkle, twinkle l __ __ __ l__ s __ __ r.
- Have students play Spelling Catch by spelling words as they throw a soft ball or beanbag to each other. They decide on the word and as they catch the ball or beanbag, they say the letter that comes next in the word.
- Have the students play the game Hangman with their spelling words. One student puts a number of blank spaces for one of the spelling words on the bottom of the paper and the other student guesses a letter. For every letter

guessed incorrectly a part of a body hanging by a rope is added, starting with a head and progressing downward.

INCREASING THE CHALLENGE

- Give words that are difficult to students who choose to take a Spelling Challenge. These Challenge words should not be part of their overall scores, but be a plus category. For example, students who spell six out of six words correctly and two Challenge words should get a score of 6, with two plus signs added for the Challenge words. This approach ensures that students are not penalized because they have not taken the Spelling Challenge or have not spelled the Challenge words correctly.

This chapter advocates a particular approach to teaching spelling to beginning writers: that spelling is best taught when the words students are spelling are linked to text they are learning to read. Before students spell, they need to develop good phonological awareness of sounds in words and alphabetic knowledge. Using a bridging device, such as sound boxes, helps students hear and records sounds in words with the purpose of having them isolate the phonemes heard and record the letters that make those phonemes, without sound boxes, as they do their independent writing. Having students familiar with word family rimes will help them learn spelling patterns and how to decode unfamiliar words through their similarity to known words. (There are also mnemonic devices to help students learn to spell, and games and exercises designed to improve visual memory, but they are not given here.)

Readers and writers improve their spelling by increasing the amount of reading and writing they do. When there is an increased output of both reading and writing, coupled with teacher expectations for careful self-editing, students' spelling will improve. To put it simply, they learn to read by reading and learn to spell through writing. Direct instruction and careful teacher monitoring of the Basic Tools are, of course, also necessary.

Harder to Spell High-Frequency Words

Aa

after
all
away
are
asked

Bb

back
because
before
by
begin

Cc

came
come
could
call
catch

Dd

day
did
dark
don't
done

Ff

for
from
find
first
friend

Gg

girl
going
goes
game
give

Hh

had
how
have
here
help

Ii

I'm
inside
I'd
idea
important

Jj

jump
just
job

Kk

kids
kind
knew
Know

Ll

lady
large
later
little

Mm

made
make
many
may

Nn

name
near
never
next

Oo

off
often
one
only

Pp

people
party
put
pretty

Rr

ride
right
really
read

Ss

said
school
shall
saw

Tt

talk
tell
than
their

Uu

under
use
until
upon

Vv

very

Ww

walk
want
work
when

Yy

yard
year
yes
you

Assessment Checklist for Word Families

1 unable to do the task
2 attempts the task with minimal ability
3 demonstrates average ability with a distinct need for further practice
4 demonstrates good ability that meets the age-appropriate standard for the task

Criteria *Dates:*						*Comments*
If given a known word, can the student make another word that is part of that word family?						
Can the student create a word-family group of four or more words from a familiar word?						
Can the student read the word-family words?						
Can the student read an unfamiliar word that belongs to a known word family?						
Can the student use the "slide" to make new words in a word family by adding different onsets to the same rime?						

Spelling Sheet

My Word to Learn	Print and circle the hard parts	Chunk the word and say it as you spell	Print it quickly	Cover your work and test yourself

6

Creating a Legible, Coherent Text

The lessons in this chapter help students create a "legible" story that makes sense and is easy to write. For this to occur, students need to know about appropriate punctuation and to have some incentive for ensuring that their written pieces demonstrate their punctuation knowledge. They need to know how to write legibly, and as they progress through school, they will likely be expected to write on lines. They need to know how to do a simple edit for punctuation and possible spelling errors, to reread what they have written, and to at least attempt to provide the reader with text that makes sense. Finally, they need to have ease in writing longer pieces of work. Building volume is not just about exercising hand muscles; it is about sustaining effort through 30-minute writing sessions.

Here is a longer story written by Dawson at the beginning of Grade 2 at Pleasant Valley Elementary School, Nanaimo, British Columbia.

ShiMPy lived inabig ocean.
a fish yelLed out Lets play tag. me too.
Sed big AL. big AL Was it.
he Coudant tag annea fish but Shrimpy
then Shrimpy Was It. he hied beahind
a Rock. and Wated just then
big AL Went CLoeS to the RocK
then big AL Was It.
all the fish sed thats no fare you gays
are out of the game. they Went to the big dea
It Was Scary but BIg AL Sed i'm-
goining to Push a green Rock in to the -
big deep. It We tumbling
big AL Push a Wite Rock into the
big deap

Translation: Shrimpy lived in a big ocean. A fish yelled out, "Let's play tag." "Me, too," said Big Al. Big Al was it. He couldn't tag another fish but Shrimpy. Then Shrimpy was it. He hid behind a rock and waited. Just then Big Al went close to the rock. Then big Al was it. All the fish said, "That's no fair. You guys are out of the game." They went to the Big Deep. It was scary but Big Al said, "I'm going to push a green rock into the big deep." It went tumbling. Big Al pushed a white rock into the Big Deep.

Printing Legibly on Lines

The rule that letters be formed from top to bottom is consistent with the way teachers want students to see print when reading: to look at print from left to right and from top of the page down. Starting letters at the top and going down also promotes fast, neat printing.

I have seen students do a wonderful job of printing legibly after being taught by teachers who espoused radically different approaches to teaching printing in the early grades. Chapter 2 discussed how to make letters and learn to print them quickly without any lines; however, some teachers start Kindergarten students printing on lined paper and it works well. Some teachers prefer interlined books; others, broadly spaced lines in blank notebooks for children to write on. Most teachers provide worksheets in science, social studies, or for literature response, with a single line for students to fill in words, answers, or writings. When students make their letters correctly shaped, with uniform sizes, with a consistent slant (if any), with just the right distance between letters, and sitting on lines, their writing is legible.

EXPLORING THE PURPOSE

The goals of printing instruction are to ensure that

- letters are formed from the top down, not from the bottom up
- letters follow a formation sequence, as shown in the Capital Letter Formation and Lowercase Letter Formation sheets, in the Appendixes
- letters have consistent sizes and heights
- letters in a word are close together without touching
- letters sit on a line — an imaginary line on blank paper — with just the tails of "tail letters" dropping below
- children develop speed and fluency in printing, easily making letters that are neither too large nor too small
- if letters have any kind of slant, they slant in the same direction

GETTING READY

Students need notebooks or lined paper and you need to provide a model either by putting lines on a whiteboard or on a chalkboard. You should also have a piece of lined chart paper ready. Plan to model each word twice, printing with a felt pen, piece of chalk, or whiteboard pen; students will use pencils.

HOW TO TEACH IT

This lesson is really about students refining their printing to make it neater and more readable. It would be taught long after children have learned how to make letter shapes correctly.

Deciding what to print is usually a fairly easy task. I like to have students print a sentence or two from the poem we use for spelling, a line of a song we are learning, an explanation of a drawing I might want them to illustrate, or a line out of their Writing Workshop notebooks. The main thing is that every child will print the same sentence.

The steps are simple:

1. Check to make sure the students are showing good writing posture, with their backs straight, their feet flat on the floor, and their bodies square to the table. Ensure, too, that their notebooks are put in the right position: at a slight angle slanting upwards to the right and centred, except for left-handed students whose books should be placed to the left of the midline.
2. Demonstrate how to print the first word on the board, emphasizing starting at the top where your chalk touches the line, and then thinking out loud about how you make the letter. For example, if making *r* on interlined chart paper, you would say, "Start on the dotted line in the middle, go down and touch the solid line, then go back up, and make a little hook on the right."

3. When it is the students' turn, print the word on the chart paper, talking them through how to make each letter as they work on their papers. Repeat for each word of the sentence. Do a word — not a letter — at a time.
4. Prompt and look for spaces between words, for letters of appropriate sizes and slant, and for correct formation. Check for proper end punctuation.

REFLECTING ON THE LEARNING

Ask the students to show you the word they think they have printed best. Give positive feedback about what they have done right.

Ask them what they know about good printing, and see if they can tell you about letters touching the line, not touching each other, and so on.

One practice I recommend is to carry a clipboard with interlined paper when you look at students' work. That way, students can see how a particular letter they had difficulty with is made and can do a quick practice on your sheet. They can then erase a letter made improperly and do it again. This is one of the few times I let them erase!

NOTES ON ASSESSMENT

Before the Lesson: This lesson should be done after the children have learned formation of all the alphabet letters, as described in Chapter 2. The students should be independently writing at least a sentence at Writing Workshop, albeit with invented spelling, which would indicate they are ready for a lesson on legible printing on lines.

During the Lesson: Check to see if a student is doing these things:

- writing between the lines, touching them but not going over them
- making the letters a consistent size
- leaving a tiny space between letters and a larger space between words

After the Lesson: After providing considerable practice with printing on lines, you may use the "Assessment of Printing" checklist (see page 126) to assess student ability to print legibly on lines.

MAKING IT SIMPLER

Highlight the Main Lines: If students are unsure about where to start and the page is lined, but not interlined, mark every second line in heavier ink to help them recognize their starting position for making letters.

Use a Spacer: Some students have difficulty in judging how much space should be between words. A narrow wooden stir-stick or Popsicle stick (about 1 cm wide), perhaps with a little face at top, can serve as a "spaceman." Students align this tool beside the word last printed, make a pencil mark, and then remove the spaceman as they write the next word. This process is somewhat unwieldy, though, so its use should be limited.

Make Bigger Spaces: Students who experience difficulty with fine motor skills may need to print larger in order to make the letters consistent sizes. By creating an interlined page with wider spaces between the lines, photocopying it on both sides of the paper, and stapling pages together with a cover, you can make a printing book that such students can succeed with.

INCREASING THE CHALLENGE

- For students who are demonstrating excellent skills printing a sentence with the careful modeling suggested in this lesson, you may want to add another line on the board for them to print on their own, without your modeling.
- Once a student has demonstrated that she or he can print quickly and accurately with a model you have given, provide a blank piece of paper and ask the student to print the sentence without using lines. The challenge is to ensure that small letters are the same size.

Learning about Capitals and Periods

Learning about punctuation begins in the first weeks of Kindergarten as the teacher creates a sentence on the board for Morning Message and talks about why there is a capital letter at the beginning of the sentence and a dot at the end. When students begin to write stories of more than one sentence or thought, attempts to punctuate their writing appropriately are expected.

HOW TO TEACH IT

Learning about capitals and periods, as well as other end punctuation, comes from many teachable moments and opportunities for modeling rather than a particular lesson. Some ideas for teaching are listed below.

Messenger game

The criterion "makes sense" can be a confusing part of the definition. What constitutes a sentence is also related to the recognition of how a sentence is constructed; what seems to be a sentence may not make literal sense. Even young students can recognize that the following is a message that might make sense to someone, if not them: *The gorkdal blisted a smeeken.* Articles, words such as *the, a,* or *an,* signal a noun or object, and an *-ed* ending signals a verb. I keep the criterion "makes sense" even though I sometimes read sentences that do not make sense to me because notions of structure and understanding are rather complicated for young children.

As mentioned in Chapter 4, students need to hear sentences before they see them and when they recognize that sentences give messages that make sense to the person hearing them, they are better able to discriminate between what is a sentence and what is not.

Taking the role of a messenger at the door, rapping loudly so everyone's attention is riveted, coming in with an important announcement, and then asking the students "Is this a message you understand?" helps them consider what a sentence is. They can put thumbs up or down. Possible messages include these: a bright red shirt; Holly has a mother; James is looking after his sister; Look!

Talk out loud

As you do modeled or interactive writing with students, make sure that you talk out loud about the message you are writing and how you start with a capital and later insert a period, which works like a little resting spot for your voice when you read. In this way students are able to tell you what comes at the beginning and end of a sentence and can place them into the text you are interactively creating.

Superimpose giant periods

It is helpful to superimpose a large period on a sticky note over any period found in a Big Book or chart story you read to students. Students will come to realize that periods can happen at the ends of lines, in the middles of lines, and sometimes quite near the beginnings of lines. This helps a lot!

Counting sentences, periods, and capitals

If you count the sentences in a page of simple text, students can begin to see about how many sentences might be on a page. When they look at a page of text and find about five periods and then look at their own similar-sized pieces of text, they should know that 2 or 11 periods aren't in the range! It is also helpful for them to count the capital letters. When they find that there are more capital letters than sentences, it is time to discuss the many uses of uppercase letters.

Dictate sentences

Beginning readers often learn to write a dictated sentence or at least the beginning of a sentence frame, such as "I like to ..." or "My favorite part is ..." Emphasizing that you will be checking for capitals and end punctuation during these times helps cement this process for students.

The unpunctuated piece of writing

Put an unpunctuated piece of writing on the board or overhead. Read it first without punctuation and pauses. Then read it again, making it sound like talking, and ask students to listen for the little stops where your voice takes a short rest. Ask them to figure out where the periods go and to remember that after a period comes a space and a capital letter. If you role-play this as a capital letter, looking down at a little period, with a gruff voice saying: "Oh, there you are! I was told to come!" this will help them remember that rule. Tell them to do the same with *their* writing.

The "two thumbs" trick

A good way for students to make sure that they haven't forgotten a period or two is to have them put one thumb on the capital and then scan for the first period. If that is four or five lines down, they have probably missed one! This quick check is a handy tool for editing.

Doing a Simple Self-Edit

Right from the very beginning of students' writing experiences, I ask them to reread what they have written. During the times when writing each word takes effort, they often need to reread so that they can determine the next word in a sentence. When students are writing stories that contain more than one idea or thought, it is time to look for some punctuation that indicates sentences. There will be attempts at capitals and periods.

Beginning writers are notorious for overusing capitals and periods, and it helps to know that this overuse is part of the natural progression towards correct punctuation use. As students become aware that a sentence needs to be a complete thought, their punctuation use becomes more standard. Although teachers often expect students to edit in partners and to revise content by looking for powerful verbs, combining short sentences, varying sentence length and verb-subject order, and questioning whether they have given the reader enough information, the focus in this section is a self-edit that looks at conventions, such as complete sentences that make sense, adequate spelling, and punctuation, as well as the coherence that comes when all sentences are on the same subject.

EXPLORING THE PURPOSE

When they first develop as writers, it is important to give students a sense of freedom about their writing. Conventions such as punctuation and spelling should not get in the way of the important work of expressing what they think and of using their imaginations to tell great stories. As students continue to write, however, they will gradually become more standard in their use of punctuation and spelling. It is the teacher's job to prompt them to apply punctuation rules and to reread their work with a special eye for ensuring they have used the proper punctuation and checked for correct spellings.

Teachers may question why this self-edit asks students to count periods, sentences, capitals, and so on. The reason is simple. Students need to recognize that simple narrative pieces have patterns. With writing that consists mostly of relatively simple sentences, there should be a period on about every other line of text and at least as many capitals as periods.

GETTING READY

My Self-Edit

Number of sentences: ______
Do a "writer's mumble." Do all sentences make sense? _____
Number of capitals: ______
Number of end punctuation marks, e.g., ., !, ? ______
Have you underlined possible spelling errors? ________

How well did you do?
Great _______ Good _______
Need to work harder ____

You will need

- a page from a Big Book or a chart story that has several properly punctuated sentences — text should be about 8 to 15 sentences long and easy for all students to read; alternatively, an overhead of a page from a book
- altered text from the Big Book written on chart paper or displayed using an overhead projector — miss periods and capitals and create a few spelling errors
- some sticky notes or correcting tape to fix errors if you are using chart paper
- a copy of the self-edit sheet (see page 123) printed out large for all students to see on the board or on chart paper

HOW TO TEACH IT

Begin the lesson by telling students you will be taking a look at the punctuation in this story and have them brainstorm what punctuation is. They usually identify periods, capitals, exclamation marks, question marks, and quotation marks. Put these marks on the board and make sure that students know what they are. Ask students to look for those marks as you read the story.

After reading, talk a bit about how writers need to check their work to make sure they have sentences that make sense and look right, that is, have capitals and some punctuation at the end. Tell them that one helpful way is to do some counting. Have the students help you count the number of sentences in the selection read. Make a note of the number on the large self-edit sheet. Then, ask students how they can tell if they are real sentences; they will usually tell you that there is a capital and a period or other punctuation mark at the end.

You may want to show them that a good way to check that the sentence makes sense is to put one thumb on the capital and the other on the period, and pretend that what you "mumble" out loud is a message like they heard in the Phoneme, Word or Sentence game (see Chapter 4). In that game, the class learns how a sentence is a message that makes sense in that listeners know something new or what to do. You may practise this with some sentences and have students decide whether each one makes sense. Then, record the number of capitals and the

Self-edit sheets, such as those at the end of the chapter, can be cut in two, put in a box near students' writing notebooks or portfolios, and with Scotch tape handily beside the box, taped into students' notebooks by the students. Students can complete them before handing in their writing pieces for teacher perusal. When students seem to have a feel for the pattern, take the sheets away and ask them to self-edit independently without counting sentences, capitals, or end punctuation marks. Use of the sheets should not last past a couple of months.

number of periods, question marks, or exclamation marks — the end punctuation marks.

Invite the students to read the selection with you, asking them to pause at each period a little longer than usual. Explain that when writers check over their writing they reread, making their voices pause at each end mark so they have time to think and answer this question, "Did this sentence make sense?"

Next, look at the "new" text, the chart-paper story that doesn't have capitals and periods, but does have some spelling errors. Close the Big Book, so students don't use it as a reference until finished.

You may want to read the new text to the students quickly and then read it again together more slowly. As you do so, listen for where your voices pause and consider putting a period there. It may be helpful to call a period a "resting spot" so that students know this is where they give their voices a little rest. Then, add a space and a capital after a period, and do other editing changes the students suggest. If they think a word is spelled incorrectly, lightly underline it with pencil.

When you and the students have sentences, "frame" them with your thumbs and have students check that they make sense by "mumbling" them under their breaths and asking, "Is this a complete message?" Together, count up sentences, capitals, and periods and record them on the enlarged self-edit sheet. Go to the underlined words and discuss where to find the correct spellings for these words. The students' suggestions usually include referring to the Word Wall, a picture dictionary, or someone who knows.

For a first lesson you can give the students the same piece of unedited text for them to do on their own, taking the overhead or chart paper reference away. (See the sample below.) This helps them get accustomed to the practice.

On another day, ask students to apply the self-edit sheet to a piece of their own writing. Talk about whether you could have a whole page of writing with only one or two capitals, one period, and so on. It is hoped they see that there needs to

Here, students first worked with the teacher to edit this piece of writing placed on the overhead projector. The class did the whole selection together. The overhead was then removed and students were given copies of the unedited piece to do on their own.

Doing an edit.

Shrimpy lived in a big ocean. He was lonely and cryed big salty tears into the big salty sea. Big Al is his freind. They playedtag. One day thay went to the Big Deep. Big Al got stuck and Shrimpy help him. Then they had a party.

Self-Edit

Number of sentences 7

Do a "writers mumble" Do all sentences make sense

Number of capitals: 12

Number of end punctuation marks, e.g. !?. 7

Have I underlined possible spelling erros. 8

be a sprinkling of capitals and periods throughout a piece of simple writing and that the number of sentences should at least match the number of end punctuation marks and capitals; through considerable practice, they will become familiar with the typical punctuation patterns in narrative text. It is helpful to post permanent reminders, such as "A capital letter likes to follow a punctuation mark. See!" or "Lightly underline words whose spellings need to be checked."

REFLECTING ON THE LEARNING

While students work on one of their pieces of text and use the self-edit checklist for counting capitals, periods, numbers of sentences, and so forth, you may ask them these questions:

- Did doing this help you find a place where you forgot some punctuation? Can you show we where?
- Can you show me how you frame a sentence to check to make sure it makes sense? What do you do when it is framed?
- Did you underline some words for spelling errors? Where will you find out how to spell those words?

NOTES ON ASSESSMENT

Before the Lesson: This lesson is done only when most of the students are independently writing texts of between 50 and 100 words and have learned to read what they have written. By now, students should be familiar with such terms as periods, capitals, sentences that make sense, commas, quotation marks, and question marks. However, reviewing what punctuation means and determining who doesn't understand that concept is essential before you teach this lesson. While field-testing this lesson, I found that my group of students did not have a clear idea of what a sentence was and so I introduced the Messenger game before proceeding with the rest of the lesson.

During the Lesson: When students are doing the edit, many will find it difficult to pause where there should be periods. It needs to be understood that determining where a sentence ends is difficult for many beginning writers. Students should grasp that capitals come right after a period, question mark, or exclamation mark in writing, and you can check whether they can do this. If you find students who have done self-edits on their work and found few capitals or end punctuation marks, ask them to check again. You may need to look together at short sample pieces of writing to see typical patterns of punctuation. They may also need to be shown how to do a writer's mumble again.

After the Lesson: Students need much prompting and experience in using devices such as a self-edit sheet to become proficient at doing a self-edit. After much practice, students can be assessed by teacher observation of their ability to edit their independent writing. Editing independent writing is a more sophisticated skill than most Grade 1 and Kindergarten students have, but it is appropriate to introduce them to the process and to have them practise it when writing text from 50 to 100 words. You can also assess their ability to edit by giving them an unedited piece of text, typical of what they would be writing independently, asking them to correct it, and counting up how many of the errors they were able to find and fix. For this kind of assessment, you need to count up the number of complete sentences and punctuation marks that should have been present in the piece and determine what percentage the student was able to find. You would also check to see how many spelling errors the student identified by underlining;

however, this formal assessment is not recommended for students in their first two years of writing.

MAKING IT SIMPLER

Focus on Less: This lesson includes looking for spelling errors, but it may be more manageable to narrow the lesson goal to teaching students about looking at sentences, capitals, and periods, and considering whether each sentence makes sense.

Spend More Time Modeling Punctuation: Put about 10 to 12 sentences of text on an overhead, circle all the end punctuation, and model reading the text with exaggerated pauses at each period, question mark, or exclamation mark. Have students read the passage in unison, doing the same thing.

All Writing in Lowercase: Some teachers ask their beginning writers not to worry about capitals or periods until they are able to write a number of complete thoughts. When they feel that students are ready to understand how capitals work in sentence structures, they go back and put capitals at the beginnings of sentences and periods at the end.

Do a Peer Edit: When students have relatively short, legible, but unedited pieces of writing from their peers to edit, they tend to take the task seriously and do it with diligence. Asking students to edit in partners can help make the process easier, as the author is available to answer questions and interpret "kidwriting."

Box It: You may want to take on the role of a capital letter looking down at the end punctuation, usually a period that sits at the end of the preceding sentence. You can ham it up with a gruff voice and a "How's it going down there, buddy? You and I, we've got to stick together! You're at the end and I'm at the beginning, but we are buddies … friends to the end!" To emphasize this relationship, have students pencil a light box around the end punctuation mark and the capital beside it on a piece of standard text, and then while they are editing.

INCREASING THE CHALLENGE

Students love to be editors. Giving them special hats, special editing pencils, or special stamps they can put on drafts that says something like "Checked!" helps them think of themselves as real editors.

- When students can do a simple self-edit, they are ready to check for more complex things. Most students have been taught that they should write about only one subject. Ask students to make sure that all their sentences pertain to only one topic — staying on topic is a natural add-on to the short list of things to look for in the self-edit sheet given. Simply prompt students to read each sentence and ask themselves, "Is this sentence about the topic I'm writing on?"
- You may photocopy a page of a student's notebook and make an overhead transparency out of it so that the whole class can edit it together. It is important to make sure that the child is not humiliated by having peers look at "errors." I often explain that this child has provided us with a wonderful opportunity to learn together and teach each other. I make sure we use everyone's book at least once.
- Provide an unedited piece of text related to a seasonal or thematic interest and have students edit it as a whole class or as an individual activity. I have provided an imaginary child's letter to Santa to be edited before it is posted to the North Pole; a letter from a somewhat illiterate witch promising a visit on Halloween, complete with edges singed from a cauldron's fire; and a letter from an Easter bunny inquiring about the best places to hide eggs. This activity makes a good early morning routine.

Writing a Longer Story — Ways to Increase Volume

Teachers of beginning writers often use the word *stories* to mean more than fiction. As other genres are introduced, they can begin using more specific terms, such as non-fiction, personal narrative, narrative, and opinion pieces; however, common practice is to use the word *stories* to describe what children write. It is generally understood not to be genre specific.

When students in the primary grades are inspired, they write long stories and demonstrate pride in the length of their pieces. "Look teacher, I wrote three pages!" is heard in numerous classrooms as students show off their masterpieces. What teacher hasn't been delighted as children come up with Chapter One at the top of their page for a chapter book? What a great beginning!

For students to write a coherent longer piece of writing with a definite beginning, middle, and end, it can be a challenge. Sometimes, it's just hard for them to write so many words. They start well, get to events in the middle, but never get to the end. Sometimes, they get distracted and the story takes off on a different, confusing tangent and they can't seem to find their way back to where they need to go. Sometimes, they have established a habit of writing only as much as will satisfy the teacher, and that is usually not a long story.

EXPLORING THE PURPOSE

This lesson should be repeated, but not often. The writing in this selection does not reflect the students' ability to be creative and doesn't provide them with the pleasure of telling their personal stories. It does, however, help students write long, coherent stories that they can be proud of.

When students write a longer piece satisfactorily and enjoy the process, the stage is set for them to repeat the experience. One of the best ways to get students to write longer, more coherent stories is to provide the scaffolding and support for them to do this successfully. Having this initial experience will encourage them to continue in a like fashion.

In this lesson, students are provided with a model that illustrates pre-planning strategies for writing a story with a beginning, middle, and end. They are given a purpose for writing, which is to re-create a story that they have been told. The teacher stresses that the product she is looking for should "tell the whole story." Expectations are set for a long story. Students are told a story which they will learn to remember through various rehearsal activities related to story details and chronology. The final task is to retell the story by writing it out on paper.

GETTING READY

A few recommended titles and authors are *The Emperor's Egg* by Martin Jenkins, *Big Al and Shrimpy* by Andrew Clements and Yoshi, and *Stellaluna* by Janell Cannon.

First, you need to find a picture book that contains a story that is easy to follow chronologically and has interesting details. Although fairy tales can work, a real test of students' ability to remember details and events will happen if they haven't heard the story before. Divide the text into four chunks that can loosely be called the beginning, the first set of events, the second set of events, and the conclusion, and put a sticky note in place to mark where each chunk begins.

The blackline master "One-Minute Sketches and Key Words," at the end of this chapter, may be useful as students' planning sheet. Students will also need a copy of "My Retelling," which I usually enlarge to an 11 by 17 piece of paper so that they have lots of room to write. The spaces on the left side can be for their illustrations or ones you have photocopied or sketched for them.

HOW TO TEACH IT

You may begin this lesson with students at the carpet. After some initial discussion about the topic, making predictions about story content, and building some incentive for listening, read them the story. After the story, have a brief discussion about what parts they liked, what they learned, and what questions they might still have.

Tell them that they are going to practise writing a long story by retelling this story on paper; however, that will be after they and you have had lots of fun doing things to help remember the important parts.

Retelling the story

One-minute sketches are exactly that: penciled sketches that show as many details as possible in one minute. The teacher says when to start, uses a watch, and says, "Pencils down" when the minute is up. These useful "thinking sketches" are not meant to be accurate drawings, but ways to visualize and remember pertinent details.

The next part of this lesson is retelling. I recommend doing this with partners, where one set of students is facing you and their partners are facing them, but away from you. The partners facing you look as you show them the first few pages as a visual reminder and mention a few key words; then, they tell the story to their partners. It is best to model a page or two of the first part of the story to the students, taking the viewing and talking position and then the listening position so that students know exactly what to do.

Students who are the listeners (the partners with their backs to you) can retell what they heard and add details that their partners who gave the story did not mention. This helps them remember the story more accurately and gives them a purpose for listening attentively.

Next, pairs shift position and the listening partners become the viewing and talking partners, telling about the next part of the story from the pictorial clues you give by showing the pages that correspond to that story chunk. This process continues through the four chunks with the students basically retelling the story to each other, and you providing visual reminders and key words.

Students then go to their desks where they will do one-minute sketches and write or read key words using the blackline master provided. This activity is done with teacher guidance. Retell the salient details of each story chunk, show them the pictures from text, and then ask them to do a one-minute sketch outlining all the details of what you have said. Then, discuss key words from the chunk they have heard, and ask them to tell the important details only and think of words they would need for a retelling. For Grade 1 students, have key words already printed on the paper and at this juncture read them together; older students could write the words independently or copy them from the board where you will have written them.

When students meet with their partners to do a task, I usually give them a time limit in order to provide incentive for them to work quickly. Although occasionally some children cannot complete the task within the time limit, it is preferable to students wasting time talking off the topic.

Go on to the next chunk, and repeat the process. When they are finished, students once more sit with their partners and retell the story orally, using their sketches and key words as guides to the chronological order and salient details.

The last part of the lesson is where students, using the planning sheets they have completed with sketches and key words, write the story, including as many details as possible. I usually give them 30 or more minutes to do this. Ideally, in this time they will fill the right side of a lined 11 by 17 page or at least write a longer piece than usual.

I have often done this lesson during a morning, but it is a departure from the 10 to 15 minutes usually devoted to Basic Tools lessons. You can split it up over several days if you wish; however, be sure to review the past day's events each time you introduce it.

At the end of their independent writing, ask students to check their planning sheets to see how many key words they have used and to do a self-edit.

REFLECTING ON THE LEARNING

In the numerous times I have done this activity, many students demonstrate more output than usual and there are many opportunities to congratulate students on their effort, their persistence, and the length of their stories. Some questions to help them reflect on their writing are these:

- Did you write a longer story than you usually do?
- What helped you write this longer story?
- Can you show me where you used the key words?
- Did you use the planning sheet? How would you make one for a story you made up yourself?

NOTES ON ASSESSMENT

Before the Lesson: This lesson is appropriate for students who have demonstrated the ability to tell a story that has at least six or seven linked ideas. Try to make sure that unfamiliar vocabulary is well explained and that the content is within the experience of the students. If you think some students may not understand some of the content, be sure to have a discussion about it, do some guided imagery, or provide visuals. For example, when using *The Emperor's Egg* by Martin Jenkins, my students and I discussed everything we knew about Antarctica and penguins, found the area on the globe, and looked at pictures of the continent.

During the Lesson: Check to see who is having difficulty retelling the story to their partners. Think about why this is happening.

- Is it because they are inattentive or uninterested in the story?
- Do they lack the language skills to explain what they know?
- Do they have difficulty remembering?

At the time, give as much support as you can, but be sure to make note of these problems. Provide opportunities for the student to do retellings where you can observe carefully to discover where the problem is.

By giving salient details just before students do their one-minute sketches, you help students think about the story again and fill in the blanks in their memories. Asking students to count how many details they have in their sketches might be one way to get them to consider whether they are using their one-minute time wisely in adding as many details as they can.

To help students become aware of how efficient a "thinking sketch" can be, at some other time have the students do three things to tell about a part of a story: draw a thinking picture in as short a time as possible, write out the details, and print a list of key words. Discuss which way gave the most information in the quickest manner.

Usually, students can come up with the key words needed, but often come up with details that are not important to the story, as well. Check to see if this is the general case and determine whether your class needs lessons on separating important from extraneous details.

After the Lesson: I have used this task as an assessment task because it tells so much about the students' use of conventions, their understanding of story chronology and structure, and their ability to sustain effort. Of course, it doesn't tell about their ability to create their own stories and to use vocabulary, imaginative details, and aspects of writing craft that fit their particular piece. What it does provide is a view of their ability to tell a known story in a legible, coherent, and logical fashion.

MAKING IT SIMPLER

Intervene with Questions: Some students find the task of retelling the story difficult and provide little information to their partners. At these times, try to intervene by asking questions, such as "Did you mention ...?" "What are some other key words to help you tell this part of the story?" The purpose is not to test students' knowledge but to ensure that partners have an opportunity to remember and to tell as much of the story as they can. Any help you can give is useful.

Provide Cue Cards: When field-testing this lesson, Terrill MacDonald made flash cards with some of the pertinent words from each chunk of the story. As one student was describing the story chunk to another, she held up cue cards as reminders of the pertinent details. This worked well and the students went on to write long and detailed stories.

Help Them Get Started: If students haven't begun this task independently within a few minutes, giving them a first sentence can be the catalyst to get them going. Few students will have difficulty beginning this writing task unless they are very reluctant writers.

Provide a Visual Display: Having some sketches or photocopied pictures set up as a visual display can help students whose own one-minute sketches may be rather devoid of useful details. Since the purpose of this lesson is to ensure the student knows what to write, providing visuals can be helpful.

Choose a Simpler Story: A simpler story will ensure that students will not have so many new details to remember. Although this makes the task easier, be cautioned that many students will not show the full range of their ability to sustain effort and tell a "long" story if the base story is short and sparse on details. I have used a relatively complex story with Grade 1 students who had little difficulty writing about the Emperor penguins in Antarctica.

INCREASING THE CHALLENGE

- I have used this same lesson up to Grade 4 with few variations and always found that it sustained students' interest and provided opportunity for them to showcase the volume of writing they could produce. Missing out one of the retellings will make this more challenging.
- For more advanced students, you could outline some expectations for dialogue or point out the criteria for good writing that you may have discussed earlier. For example, have clear expectations for students to follow a story outline with setting, character introductions, problem, plot, and resolution, if students are familiar with those aspects of story grammar.

An example of "One-Minute Thinking Sketches" comes from Alyssa, and an example of a longer story comes from Lucas. Both Grade 2 students did their work based on *Big Al and Shrimpy*, by Andrew Clements and Yoshi, in September of the school year at Pleasant Valley Elementary School, Nanaimo, British Columbia.

One-Minute Thinking Sketches and Key Words

One- Minute Sketch	Key Words:
	Shrimpy smart small lonely Big Al tag
	friend places Big Deep scary edge stuck tumbling
	everyone help couldn't lantern orders pulled loose
	around follow party guest ideas

Translation: Shrimpy lived in a big ocean. Shrimpy and all of the fish played tag. Shrimpy tagged Big Al and Big Al tagged Shrimpy. All of the fish said, "You keep tagging each other." And that's how they became friends. They went to the Big Deep. Shrimpy said, "Can you push a rock down?" Big Al puffed his self up and pushed and pushed a green rock down. Big Al said, "I'll push a bigger rock down." He puffed his self up and pushed a big rock down and fin caught in the rock. Shrimpy told the other fish. The fish came to help Big Al. They got Big Al out. They had a big party.

Shrimpy lives in a big ocean.
Shrimpy and all of the fish
Plad tag. Shrimpy taged
big al and big al taged
Shrimpy. al of the fish sed
you keep tagin ecotr.
and tats has tay bekam
friends. thay went to
the big deep Shrimpy sed
can you push a roke down
big al pufft his self up
and pushd and pushd a
green rock down big al
sed ill push a biigre roke
down he pufft his self up
and push a big rocke down
and his fine in the the
roce shrinpy tolt the fish
the fish came to big al
tay got big al out tay had

This example of "One-Minute Thinking Sketches" became the basis of the retelling shown on page 122.

One-Minute Thinking Sketches and Key Words

One- Minute Sketch	Key Words:
	Windy Antarctica
	egg Emperor Penguin
	mom sed dad egg siting
	mom trumpets wistler

Here is a retelling of *The Emperor's Egg* by Martin Jenkins, by Haven, a Grade 2 student at Ladysmith Primary School, Ladysmith, British Columbia, in October.

Translation: There is a huge island. It is Antarctica. It is the coldest and windiest island. It is very big. There is an animal here on Antarctica, the Emperor penguin. What is that on his feet? An egg. The mom went to the sea to eat and swim. The dad keeps the egg warm. When it is windy the Emperor penguins huddle together. Then the egg hatches to a chick. Then he has two jobs. He has to feed and keep warm. But how does he make food? He has a pouch at the bottom of his throat. It's milky formula he almost out (?) it. Then the mom comes back home. Then the mom and dad trumpet and the chick whistles. It is Mom's turn to feed the chick. She makes herself sick and throws it up and the dad waves good-bye. And he goes to sea to eat and swim.

There is a huge island
it is Antorctica. It is the
Cold's and windy's island.
It is vary big there is
a anmull here on Antarctica
the Emper peguin. Wate
is that on his fet a ?
egg the mom whent to
the sea to eat and swim.
The dad keps the egg
warm. wene is windy
the Emper penguins
huddle together. Then the
egg hachs to a chick.
then he has two jobs
he has to feed and kep
warm. but howe dusse
he mack food he has
a powche at the botum
uove his throte its mecky
formeya he omost out
uove it. Than the mom
coms back home. than the
mom and dad trumpet and
and the chick whistle.
It is mom's trne
to feed the chick.
she macks her selfe
sick and thros it up
and the dad waves
good-bye. and he gowse
to sea to eat and swim.

My Self-Edit

Number of sentences: ______________________________

Do a "writer's mumble." Do all sentences make sense? ______________

Number of capitals: ______________________________

Number of end punctuation marks, e.g., ., !, ? ______________

Have you underlined possible spelling errors? ______________

How well did you do?

Great ________ Good ________ Need to work harder ______________

My Self-Edit

Number of sentences: ______________________________

Do a "writer's mumble." Do all sentences make sense? ______________

Number of capitals: ______________________________

Number of end punctuation marks, e.g., ., !, ? ______________

Have you underlined possible spelling errors? ______________

How well did you do?

Great ________ Good ________ Need to work harder ______________

One-Minute Thinking Sketches and Key Words

One-Minute Sketch	Key Words

My Retelling of ______________________________

Illustrations may be made here.

Assessment of Printing

1 unable to do the task
2 attempts the task with minimal ability
3 demonstrates average ability with a distinct need for further practice
4 demonstrates good ability that meets the age-appropriate standard for the task

Criteria *Dates:*							*Comments*
Has paper in appropriate position							
Sits with appropriate posture for good printing (back straight, feet flat on floor)							
Holds pencil with appropriate grip							
Pencil pressure is appropriate (not too hard or too soft)							
Writes on the lines							
Leaves appropriate spaces between letters							
Leaves appropriate spaces between words							
Writing is legible							
All letters slant in the same direction							
Uppercase and lowercase letters are uniform in size							
Letters are formed with top-to-bottom formations							

Recommended Resources

Adams, Marilyn Jager, Barbara R. Foorman, Ingvar Lundberg, and Terri Beeler. *Phonemic Awareness in Young Children: A Classroom Curriculum.* Baltimore, MD: Paul H. Brookes Publishing, 1998.

Brailsford, Anne, and Tony Stead. *Literacy Place for the Early Years Writing Guide, Grade 1.* Markham, ON: Scholastic, 2005.

Calkins, Lucy. *The Nuts and Bolts of Writing.* Portsmouth, NH: Heinemann, 2003.

Clay, Marie. *An Observation Survey of Early Literacy Achievement.* Portsmouth, NH: Heinemann, 1993.

Ditzel, Resi Jo. *Great Beginnings.* Portland, ME: Stenhouse, 2000.

Earl, Lorna, and Steven Katz. *Rethinking Classroom Assessment with Purpose in Mind.* Manitoba: Western and Northern Canadian Protocol for Collaboration in Education, 2007. www.wncp.ca.

Gear, Adrienne. *Reading Power.* Markham, ON: Pembroke, 2006.

Lucas, Bill, and Alistair Smith. *Help Your Child to Succeed.* Markham, ON: Pembroke, 2004.

McCarrie, Andrea, Gay Su Pinnell, and Irene C. Fountas. *Interactive Writing.* Portsmouth, NH: Heinemann, 1992.

Miller, Debbie. *Reading with Meaning.* Portland, ME: Stenhouse, 2002.

Morrow, Lesley Mandel. *The Literacy Center.* Portland, ME: Stenhouse, 2002.

Ottley, Pamela, and Lorna Bennett. *Launch into Reading Success through Phonological Awareness Training.* Vancouver: Creative Curriculum Inc., 1997.

Palmer, Sue, and Ros Bayley. *Early Literacy Fundamentals.* Markham, ON: Pembroke, 2005.

Pinnell, Gay Su, and Irene C. Fountas. *Word Matters: Teaching Phonics and Spelling in the Reading/Writing Classroom.* Portsmouth, NH: Heinemann, 1998.

Reid, Janine, and Betty Schultze with Ulla Petersen. *What's Next for This Beginning Writer?* Markham, ON: Pembroke, 2005.

Rowsell, Jennifer. *Family Literacy Experiences.* Markham, ON: Pembroke, 2006.

Schultze, Betty, and Janine Reid. *Writers Alive! for Grade One.* Vancouver, BC: VSB Media and Library Services, 2004.

Stead, Tony. *Is That a Fact? Teaching Nonfiction Writing K–3.* Portland, ME: Stenhouse, 2002.

Wells, Jan, and Janine Reid. *Writing Anchors.* Markham, ON: Pembroke, 2004.

Appendixes

The appendixes that follow are all reproducible pages. The Letter Formation sheets show freehand printing as teachers and students would do.

Generic Assessment Checklist *129*
Lowercase Letter Formation *130*
Uppercase Letter Formation *131*

Generic Assessment Checklist

Assessing the basic skill of ____

Year ______________

1 unable to do the task
2 attempts the task with minimal ability
3 demonstrates average ability with need for further practice
4 good ability — meets age-appropriate standards for the task

Description of proficiency levels, with 1 the lowest and 4 the highest

Date Assessed: *Names of Students*										

Lowercase Letter Formation

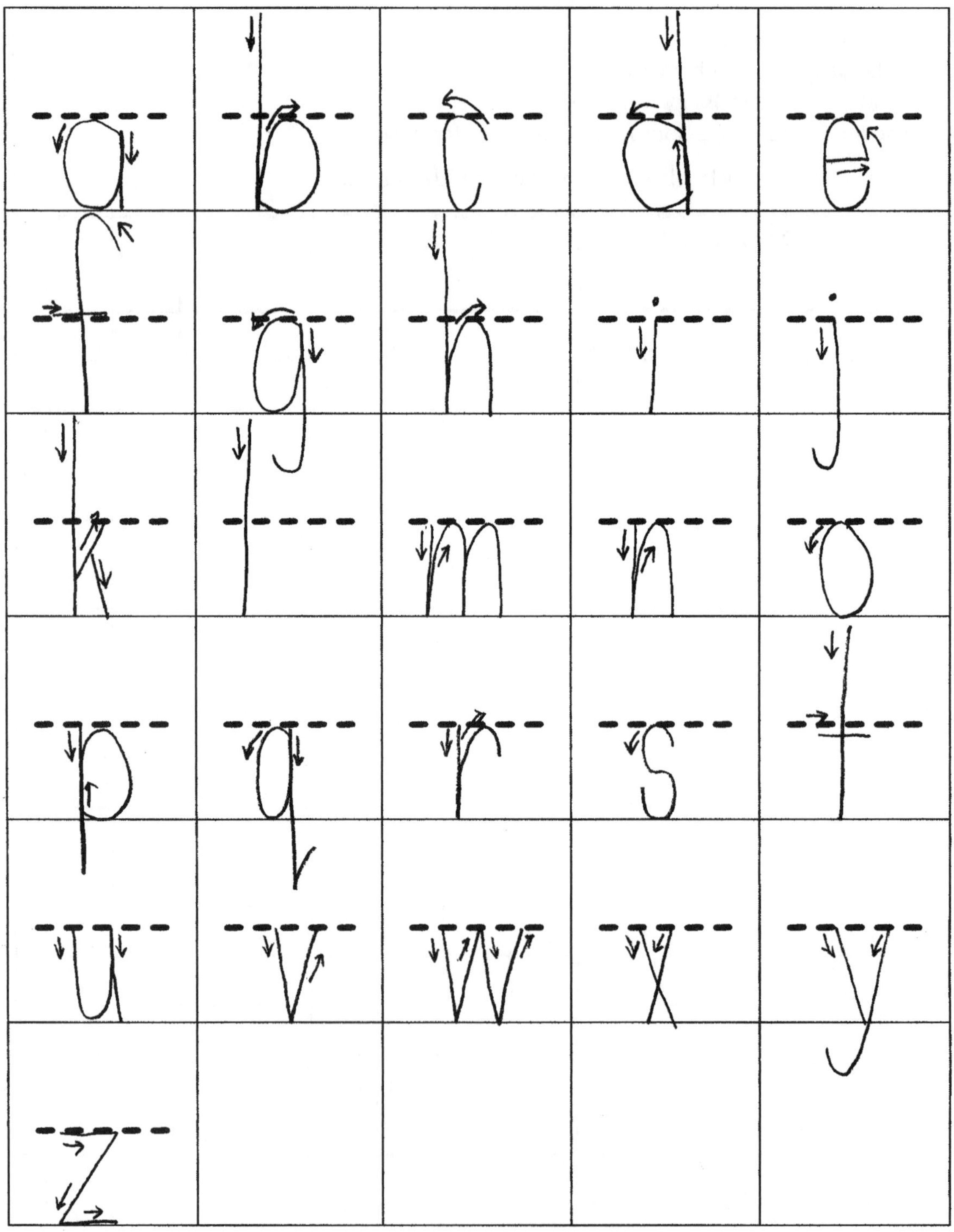

Uppercase Letter Formation

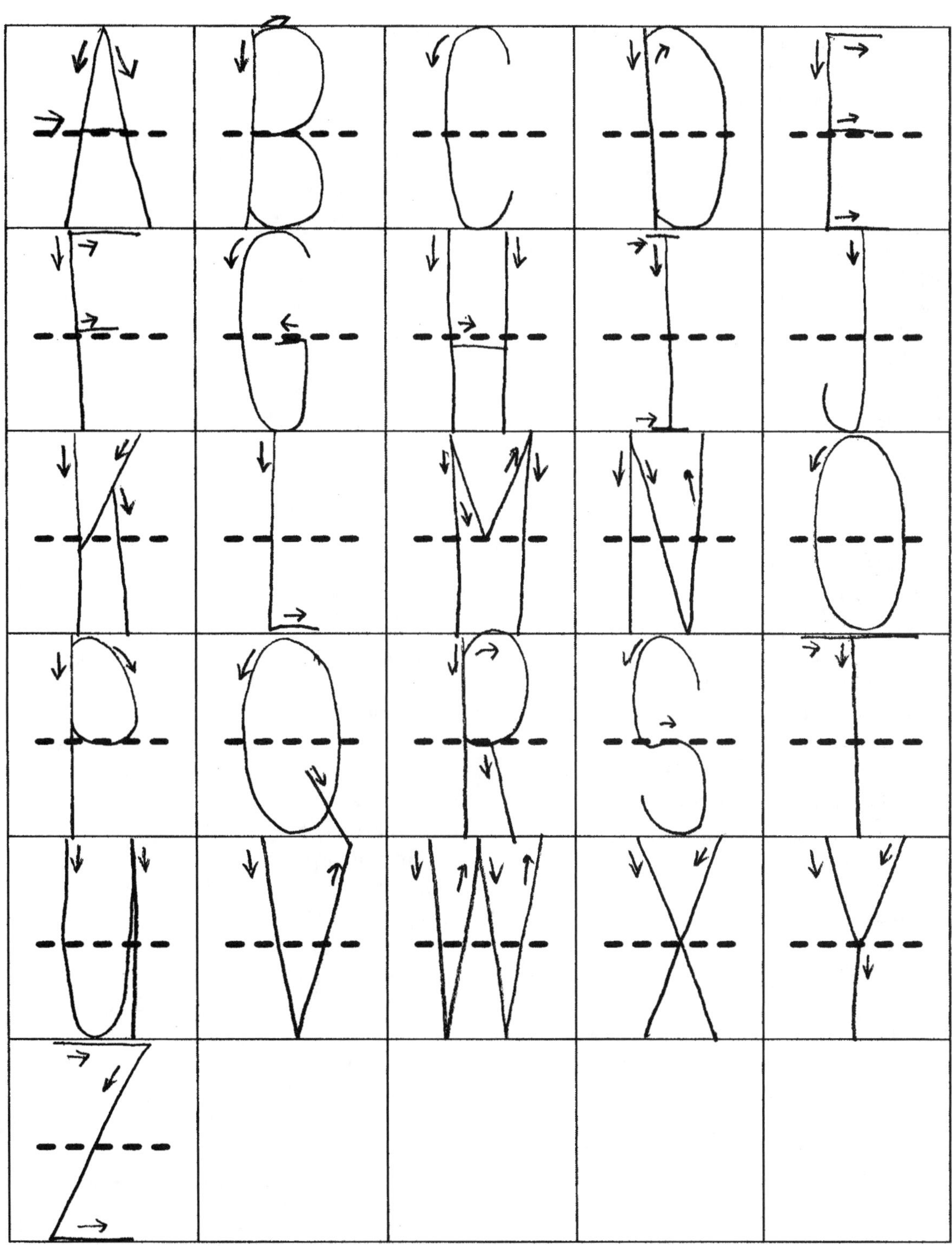

Index

Alphabet
- Assessment checklist for recognizing, 41, 55
- Checking recognition, 41, 56
- Identifying and making letters of, 37–56
- Letters of, 5, 14, 43
- Tools, 6

Alphabet picture books, 46–53
- Activities, 47–48
- List, 48
- Teaching, 47

Alphabet raps or jives, 46–53
- Example, 49–53

Alphabet stories, 38–42
- Assessment, 41
- Increasing the challenge, 42
- Preparation, 38
- Purpose, 38
- Reflecting on learning, 40
- Simplifying, 41–42
- Teaching, 38–39

Anchor words, 58, 60, 62

Assessment, 14–15
- Basic skills, 14–15
- Checklist for putting pencil to paper, 36
- General checklist, 26, 129
- Letters of the alphabet, 14
- Notes on, 20, 25–26, 31–32, 41, 46, 73–74, 76–77, 80, 84–85, 94–95, 98, 102–3, 110, 115–16, 119
- Phonetic matches, 15
- Printing, 110, 126
- Self, 25–26
- Spelling and use of conventions, 14–15
- Whether students can isolate beginning sounds, 88

Basic writing tools, 5, 9, 16, 57–69, 86, 91
- Alphabetic, 6
- Incorporating into routines and play, 57–69
- Phonemic, 6
- Using, 15
- When to teach, 10

Building volume, 108, 117–20

Bumping game (blending two phonemes), 78–81, 83
- Assessment, 80
- Increasing the challenge, 81
- Preparation, 78
- Purpose, 78
- Reflecting on learning, 80
- Simplifying, 80–81
- Teaching, 79–80

Capitals and periods, 111–12
- Counting sentences, periods, and capitals, 112
- Dictating sentences, 112
- Messenger game, 111
- Superimposing giant periods, 111
- Talking out loud, 111
- Teaching, 111
- “Two thumbs” trick, 112
- Unpunctuated writing, 112

Carpet instruction, 11, 44

Centres
- Alphabet, 69
- Blocks, 64, 65–66
- Easels, 64, 67–68
- Home, 64, 66–67
- Literacy, 65, 68–69, 97
- Post office, 68
- Sharing after, 69
- Students–teacher, 69
- Teaching, 11
- Writing, 68
- Writing in, 64–65, 99

Classroom setup, 10–11

Cloze activities, 58, 63, 103
- Communicating through, 62
- Introducing, 58–59

Comparison, 20

Compound words, 77

Consonant Stories, 38, 40

Creating legible, coherent text, 108–22

Digraphs, 86

Directed drawing, 28, 29

Direct instruction, 1, 15, 104

Dolch list of common words, 99

Drawing/making simple pictures, 28–34, 67
- Assessment, 31–32
- Increasing the challenge, 32
- Preparation, 29
- Purpose, 28

Reflecting on learning, 31
Shapes, 29
Simplifying, 32
Teaching, 29–30

Elkonin boxes, 81–86
Assessment, 84–85
Increasing the challenge, 86
Move It and Say It, 83
Preparation, 82–83
Purpose, 82
Reflecting on learning, 84
Say It Slow and Write It, 83–84
Simplifying, 85–86
Teaching, 83
Emergent learners, 15, 62
English Language Learners (ELLs), 13–14

Fine motor skills, 5, 25, 57, 66, 110
Developing, 21

Generic Assessment Checklist, 26, 129
Ghost Talk, 9, 74–78
Assessment, 76–77
Increasing the challenge, 78
Preparation, 75
Purpose, 75
Reflecting on learning, 76
Simplifying, 77–78
Teaching, 75–76
Wordy, 75, 90
Graphophonemic skills, 10
Gross motor movement, 18
Guided reading groups, 92, 95

Hand over hand, 25, 27, 41
Harder to spell high-frequency words, 91, 105
Holding a pencil correctly, 18–21
Assessment, 20
Increasing the challenge, 21
Preparation, 18
Purpose, 18
Simplifying, 20–21
Teaching, 18–19
Home
Keeping in touch with, 15–16

I Spy, 44, 64

Learning
Enhancing, 69
Involving all students in, 12–13
Labeling, 20
Play, 57
Reflecting on, 25, 31, 40, 46, 73, 76, 80, 84, 94, 97–98, 102, 110, 115, 118
Spelling, 91–107
Teacher's attitude toward, 9
Learning environment, 7
Letter formation, 5, 16
Lowercase, 109, 130
Uppercase, 109, 131
Letter shapes
Capital and lowercase, 39, 41, 60
Recognizing, 39, 41, 46

Making observations, 9
Matching, 84
Modeling, 8–9, 24
Copying, 22
Steps, 8
Writing, 59, 111
Morning Message, 8, 10, 57–64, 74, 76, 94, 99, 111
Description, 57–58
Stage four: communicating through cloze, 62
Stage one: two lines of print, 59
Stage three: guiding practice, 60–61
Stage two: introducing cloze, 59–60
Ways to provide variety, 62–64
Move It and Say It, 83, 98, 100, 101, 102
My Retelling, 117, 125
My Self-Edit, 113, 123
My Turn, Your Turn, 23, 29

Non-speech sounds, 71, 72

Observation, 9
One Minute Thinking Sketches and Key Words, 117, 120,124
One-to-one correspondence, 84
Onset, 95–99

Partner Talk, 12, 13
Partner work, 12–13, 118
Pencil skills, 5, 16
Assessment checklist, 36
Drawing/making simple pictures, 17, 28–34
Holding a pencil correctly, 17, 18–21
Printing names, 17, 22–28
Putting pencil to paper, 17–36
Phoneme, word, or sentence?, 71–74
Assessment, 73–74
Game, 72–73, 113

Increasing the challenge, 74
Preparation, 71
Purpose, 71
Reflecting on learning, 73
Simplifying, 74
Teaching, 71–72
Phonemes, 5, 6, 37, 38, 58, 70–90, 91, 96, 101, 102, 104
Blending (bumping) two together, 78–81
Comparing to words and sentences, 71–74
Isolating, 9, 76, 85, 93
Separating in simple words (ghost talk), 74–78
Tools, 6
Words with three, 76, 77, 83, 86
Words with two, 75, 78–81, 83, 85, 86
Phonemic awareness, 70–90, 104
Checklist for skills, 87
Phonetic matches, 15
Popcorn words, 92
Position words, 70, 84
Power of onset and rime, 95–99
Assessment, 98
Increasing the challenge, 99
Preparation, 96
Purpose, 96
Reflecting on learning, 97–98
Simplifying, 98–99
Teaching, 96–97
Working with word families, 95–99
Practice
Guided, 8, 60–61
Independent, 8
Printing, 9, 16
Assessment, 110, 126
Legible, 109–11
Preparing students for, 19
Printing legibly on lines, 109–11
Assessment, 110
Increasing the challenge, 111
Preparation, 109
Purpose, 109
Reflecting on learning, 110
Simplifying, 110
Teaching, 109–10
Printing My Name, 23, 35
Printing names, 22–28, 92
Assessment, 25–26
Daily sign-in, 25–28
Increasing the challenge, 27–28
Preparation, 23
Purpose, 22–23
Reflecting on learning, 25
Simplifying, 26–27
Teaching, 23–24
Using buddies to help students, 24
Yes/no graph, 24
Punctuating text/punctuation, 58, 113, 114, 115, 116
Learning about, 111–12
Modeling, 116

Read It! Write It!, 92–95
Assessment, 94–95
Increasing the challenge, 95
Post-lesson suggestions, 94
Preparation, 93
Purpose, 92–93
Reflecting on learning, 94
Simplifying, 95
Teaching, 93–94
Recognizing different levels of readiness, 9–10
Recording progress, 9
Reflecting out loud, 7, 25, 111
Repetition, 7, 95
Retelling, 118, 119, 120
Rhyming words, 71, 95, 96
Rime, 95–99
Routine, 57

Say It Slow and Write It, 83–84, 101, 102
Scaffolding, 9
Self-edit (simple), 112–16
Assessment, 115–16
Increasing the challenge, 116
Preparation, 113
Purpose, 113
Reflecting on learning, 115
Simplifying, 116
Teaching, 113–15
Sentence strips, 67, 94
Setting appropriate expectations, 13–14
Modified, 32
Sight vocabulary, 91, 92, 96, 102
Six alphabet stations, 43–46
Assessment, 46
At the carpet, 44
Designing focus letter necklace or bracelet, 45
Finding focus letter in names, 44
Focus letter sort, 45
Making a picture out of focus letter, 44
Making focus letter booklet, 45
Making focus letter into cookie, 44–45
Preparation, 43–44
Purpose, 43

Reflecting on learning, 46
Teaching, 44–45
Sketches, 118, 119
Sound boxes, 81–86, 89, 101, 104
Sound–symbol matches, 38, 46, 48, 58, 60, 70–90
Spelling, 91–107
Creating a weekly list, 99–104
Phonetic, 101
Text-based ideas, 99
Spelling Challenge, 103, 104
Spelling rules, 91
Spelling sheet, 107
Stations, 43
Six alphabet, 43–46
Students
Motivated, 15
Struggling, 13
Syllables, 101

Teaching
Basic writing skills, 6–9
Cardinal rule, 9
Drawing / making simple pictures, 28–34
Holding a pencil, 18–21
Printing names, 22–28
Teaching centre, 11
Teaching basic writing skills, 6–9
Learning by experiencing success, 7–8
Learning to write through writing, 6–7
Modeling as part of direct instruction, 8–9
Tracing, 27

Unison responses, 75–76

Vowel Stories, 38, 39, 54

Weekly spelling list, 99–104
Assessment, 102–3
Increasing the challenge, 104
Preparation, 100
Purpose, 100
Reflecting on learning, 102
Simplifying, 103–4
Teaching, 100–102
Word families, 91, 95–99
Assessment checklist, 106
Simpler, 99
Working with, 95–99
Word Walls, 91, 94, 99
Writers
Beginning, 6, 7, 112
Writing
Basic conventions, 7
Basic tools, 5, 9, 10, 57–69
Beliefs about teaching basic skills, 6–9
Children learn to write through, 6–7
Developing competency, 5
Direct instruction, 10
Dominant hand, 18
Emergent, 62, 75
Left-handed, 27
Modeling, 59
Path to ability, 9–10
Using models to further, 7
Writing longer stories, 117–20
Assessment, 119
Increasing the challenge, 120
Preparation, 117
Purpose, 117
Reflecting on learning, 118
Retelling the story, 118
Simplifying, 119–20
Teaching, 117
Writing process, 5
Writing workshop, 6, 7, 10, 16, 28, 82, 84, 94, 95, 99, 109, 110

Zone of proximal development, 7, 8

Acknowledgments

This book had its origins in the work done by myself and others in the Early Literacy Project of the Vancouver School District as we explored what lessons needed to be taught to beginning writers. Since then, with the help and encouragement of several interested teachers, new ideas have been added and old ones improved. I would like to acknowledge the following colleagues for their help in making suggestions, reading and editing the manuscript, and believing that this project was worthwhile. Thank you, Janine Reid, Lisa Sahli-Graham, Carolyn Holland, Paddy Waymark, Carol Jepson, and Donna Klockers, for your time and invaluable assistance.

I give special thanks to Heather Gray of Gabriola Island for the encouragement, insights, and concrete suggestions she gave on the many mornings we met to talk about teaching beginning students. She was an invaluable source of support. The other person I especially acknowledge is my daughter Kristine West-Sells who, as a Kindergarten teacher, kept reassuring me that this book was necessary and valuable. Not only did she thoughtfully read and critique my writing, her enthusiasm kept me positively on track.

Numerous teachers in the Nanaimo School District opened their classrooms so I could do some teaching and gather student samples. The teachers at Pleasant Valley Elementary School were Cathie Bell, Gail Thompson, Leslie Raines, and Lesley Carter. At Ladysmith Primary School, Terrill MacDonald, Sandra Pollmer, and Teri Hooper tried out lessons, gave me valuable feedback, and provided student samples. Thank you for your generous support.